A Rogues' Gallery

VICTORIAN PRISONERS OF
GLOUCESTER GAOL

A Rogues' Gallery

Elizabeth Jack

The
History
Press

First published 2009

The History Press
The Mill, Brimscombe Port
Stroud, Gloucestershire, GL5 2QG
www.thehistorypress.co.uk

ISBN 978 0 7524 5129 9

Typesetting and origination by The History Press
Printed in Great Britain

CONTENTS

ACKNOWLEDGEMENTS

All photographs used in the book are reproduced with the kind permission of Gloucestershire Archives.

First and foremost, I must thank the staff of Gloucestershire Archives for their kindness, help and advice during my research, particularly Paul Evans and Vicky Thorpe. It has been much appreciated.

Equally important has been the support and encouragement given to me by my late husband, Alan, and by my daughter and son. They are a constant source of inspiration to me.

INTRODUCTION

Few persons who have ever sat for a portrait can have felt anything but inferior while the process is going on.

Anthony Powell

This must undoubtedly have been the case for those men, women and children pictured here during their stay in Gloucester Gaol, although at least their photographic experience was over fairly quickly. Whilst most portraits made in the late Victorian and early Edwardian period were of the rich and famous, few pictures existed of the lower classes. So, when seeking a photograph of an ancestor several years ago, I was delighted to come across the four albums of prisoners' photographs held in Gloucestershire Archives – a veritable treasure trove!

The photographs, as could be expected after more than 100 years, are not all in the best of condition and have been difficult to copy, but they provide a fascinating glimpse of life back then; a life seemingly spent on the bread line for most of these inmates. Many photographs are not in a suitable state to be reproduced here but all have been taken again and preserved for the future. Those images that are shown here, less than half of the total, have been cropped to tidy the edges up a little but no alterations have been made to any of the facial features, so what appears here is a 'warts and all' portrait of the inmate at the time.

It should be noted that about half of the prisoners who had their picture taken in Gloucester Gaol did not actually come from the county of Gloucestershire itself but from all corners of the United Kingdom and, indeed, the whole world. Most of the inmates were from the working classes, though there were a few middle class and professional people as well. They have been unusually difficult to trace through the normal resources of censuses and birth, marriage and death indexes. This is partly, I guess, through a desire to avoid notice of the authorities and also due to the frequent use of aliases.

Most of the crimes committed were petty offences, crimes which would not involve a custodial sentence today; those prisoners who committed more serious crimes were sent to the penitentiary instead. Sentences ranged from a few days to a couple of years and almost all of them involved hard labour. Very few adults were treated to lashes from the birch rod, but many of the children had to undergo this punishment as well as the incarceration and hard labour, a sad state of affairs.

The images show the prisoners experiencing all kinds of emotions: fear, apprehension, nervousness, indifference; some are bemused and depressed, others defiant and cheerful. Together with details of their crimes and some background information, we get a glimpse of what life must have been like for many of the poorer people in society just over 100 years ago. It is only when the whole collection of pictures and the details of the relevant crimes are read that we can understand the poverty and degradation that many of our ancestors experienced.

Disappointingly, I did not find any of my own ancestors in the albums but, having been born and bred in Gloucester, I did find some of the images vaguely familiar.

Elizabeth Jack
June 2009

one

THE PHOTOGRAPHS

Photography started in the mid–1840s and, soon afterwards, some prison governors experimented with the new facility to take pictures of the men, women and children held in their gaols, but it wasn't until 1863 when a Select Committee of the House of Commons recommended the photographing of all prisoners that it became commonplace. Recognition of previous offenders was difficult at that time, so a photograph helped to identify those with an existing criminal record, especially those using an alias; fingerprinting did not become available until the end of the Victorian era. The governor of the County Gaol in Gloucester at the time, Henry Kenneth Wilson, supported the idea of photographing prisoners, but either he restricted its use to certain reoffenders only or any other albums produced during that period have been lost over time.

Gloucestershire Archives has four albums of photographs of prisoners (Ref. Q/Gc/10/1 to Q/Gc/10/4) starting in 1870 and ending in 1935, though the period covered by them is very patchy. One album also contains some loose pages with photographs obviously from another missing album and one (Ref: Q/Gc/10/3) is not yet available to the public as it is covered by the 100 year disclosure rule.

The first album of photographs of prisoners held in Gloucester Gaol was produced between 4 April and 9 July 1870. It is entitled 'County Prison: Return of Habitual Criminals' and, inside, clarified as the Duplicate Return made to the Registrar of Habitual Criminals, 4 Whitehall Place, London.

On 4 April 1870, the governor, Henry Wilson, wrote in his journal:

Mr Thomas the photographer attended and took the photographs of 13 Habitual Criminals tried during the past sessions and assizes.

Four days later, he recorded:

Photographs and descriptions of 2 Habitual Criminals when discharged on 19th inst. sent to the London Office, Chief Constable of the County, Chief Constables of Wiltshire and Worcestershire; also to the Governor of Bristol Gaol.

On the last day of April, the governor stated:

> Mr Thomas the photographer came and took the photographs of all prisoners to be discharged between the 1st and 14th of May 1870 who have been committed for offences coming under the 1st Schedule of the Habitual Criminals Act.

'Mr Thomas the photographer' was one Abraham Thomas, who worked from premises in College Green, Gloucester, situated not far from the County Gaol.

This first album consists of 282 records of prisoners plus an index. Each entry occupies one page, listing the prisoner's name, birthplace, marital status, occupation, his or her age and destination on discharge, plus an excellent physical description of each person including height, colour of hair and eyes, complexion and any other distinguishing marks, obviously so that the criminal could be recognised again. On the crime that had been committed, the offence, place and date of conviction and sentence were recorded, together with details of some earlier convictions, if there were any.

Exactly 200 of these records do not have a photograph attached to them, but the first five entries do, and the final records in the album as well. It is not completely clear why pictures were taken of some prisoners but not others. Clearly the title of 'Habitual Criminals' indicates the fact that they were reoffenders, but many of the entries do not refer to any previous convictions, and some that do contain information on former crimes don't have any photographs.

The dubious honour of being the first in the album falls to one Henry Winniatt. Henry was born in the parish of St Augustine the Less in Bristol about 1826, the son of John and Mary Winniatt. The 1841 census shows a fourteen-year-old Henry living with his parents and five siblings in Mark Lane. His father, John, was then a flyman, who drove a one horse, two-wheeled light carriage. By 1851, John had become a fly proprietor and his son, Henry, a coachman.

After ten more years, Henry can be found still in a single state, living in Money Street with his parents, though all his siblings have moved on. At this time, both father and son were cab drivers but by the time Henry was in Gloucester Gaol in 1870, he was calling himself a groom. Horses obviously played a big part in his life.

His early criminal career began, according to the record, in 1864 when he was convicted in Bristol of stealing a drawer, for which he was sentenced to twenty-one days of hard labour. Less than a year later, he was again convicted in Bristol, this time of stealing a horsecloth. His sentence was more severe this time, being double his previous one.

The crime for which Henry was sentenced to Gloucester Gaol at the Gloucester Quarter Sessions was stealing an overcoat, 'value of £1 10s, the property of C.J. Cryer at Wotton under Edge on 24 August 1869'. For that offence, he was given six months hard labour and seven years under police supervision.

From his record, we know that Henry was 5ft 5in tall, had light brown hair, hazel eyes and a fresh complexion. A thorough examination of the prisoner enabled the warder to record that Henry also had a scar on his forehead and each groin, that he had a fresh mole on his chest, eruptions on his body and presumably had a bunion, as it stated that his large toe joint had grown out.

Henry Winniatt, 16 April 1870.

Alfred Morgan, 16 April 1870.

What happened to Henry when he left gaol is not known, but he did not live to a great age, dying in the Clifton district of Bristol in 1877 at the stated age of fifty-three.

The next four entries are for Alfred Morgan, Joseph Kendall, Samuel George Merrett and James Hyde. The last three were all considered to be serious offenders, sentenced to seven years of penal servitude each and sent off to Pentonville Prison.

Alfred Morgan was a thirty-nine-year-old married painter from Cheltenham, convicted of stealing nine knives and sentenced on 20 October 1869 at Gloucester Quarter Sessions to six months hard labour, followed by seven years under police supervision; he was 5ft 4in tall, with light brown hair, light grey eyes and a fresh complexion. Alfred had scars on his left side and forehead and contraction of his left elbow. The record also stated that he was nearly bald. Although his picture shows an inoffensive looking man, Alfred had previously been convicted of assault in 1866 and stealing a waistcoat in 1865.

Joseph Kendall was a thirty-two-year-old labourer from Boddington convicted of housebreaking. Joseph was tried at the Epiphany Sessions at Gloucester on 5 January 1870 and was given a sentence of seven years penal servitude and seven years under police supervision. His previous record showed convictions going back more than twenty years, to 1848 when he was found guilty of stealing lead. Other crimes included poaching, stealing shirts, fruit and carpets and being caught on premises for an unlawful

Clockwise from bottom left
James Hyde, 16 April 1870.

Joseph Kendall, 16 April 1870.

Samuel George Merritt, 16 April 1870.

purpose. Joseph, described as 5ft 7in tall and having brown hair, grey eyes and a light complexion, had a cut on his left wrist and white flesh marks on his neck and hips. He was sent to Pentonville Prison on 18 April 1870 to serve his sentence.

Samuel George Merrett was aged twenty-two and a cloth-worker from Stroud who was convicted of stealing boots at the Epiphany Sessions in Gloucester on 5 January 1870 and sentenced to seven years of penal servitude and seven years under police supervision. He was removed to Pentonville Prison on 18 April 1870. Samuel, a single man, was described as having brown hair, blue eyes and a fresh complexion. He was 5ft 3in tall with scars on his forehead and a fracture of his left thigh. His previous convictions included stealing three pigs in 1865 and burglary two years later. The governor wrote in his journal:

Has been tried for felony in Wiltshire and Leeds and has been a thief from boyhood.

James Hyde was obviously a hardened criminal with a long record of previous convictions. At the age of thirty-four, James gave his birth place as Cheltenham and said that he was married and working as a labourer. On 21 October 1869, at the Gloucester Michaelmas Sessions, James was charged with, of all things, stealing pigs' cheeks! When he was found guilty, he was sentenced, like the previous two prisoners, to seven years penal servitude followed by seven years under police supervision. James had light brown hair, grey eyes and a fresh complexion. At 5ft 4in tall, James had a scar on his right eyebrow, one on his right cheek and left groin and a fracture of his right leg. But by far his worst medical condition was that he was blind in his left eye.

The following 200 entries in the register are without photographs. Most of their crimes consisted of stealing something relatively minor, such as butter, forks, ribbon, a bag, and bedding, with a few instances of minor wounding or assault; cases which today would merit a community service order, rather than the incarceration with hard labour that was meted out to the Victorian prisoners. It is in the final seventy-seven photographic records of the first album that we discover both the youngest prisoner, aged seven, and the oldest, aged eighty; more of these records later.

The second album, Q/Gc/10/2, contains nothing but photographs taken between 1899 and 1915, of which only those taken before 1909 have been copied, due to the 100 year disclosure rule. There are several loose leaves tucked inside this volume which obviously came from another album originally. Usually, there are nine or twelve pictures on a page. Information has been collected on many of these criminals giving their personal details and the crime they committed.

The final album to have been used is Q/Gc/10/4. This covers part of the same period as Album 2, with photographs taken between 1882 and 1906. All of the photographs in this final album have nothing but the name and number of the prisoner and the date of the photograph written on them. Like the second album, these photographs are usually arranged twelve to a page. Very little extra information has yet been located on these convicts, apart from the occasional alias.

The photographs have suffered during the past 100 years. Some have faded or are rather dark, most have buckled where they have been stuck to the pages of the albums,

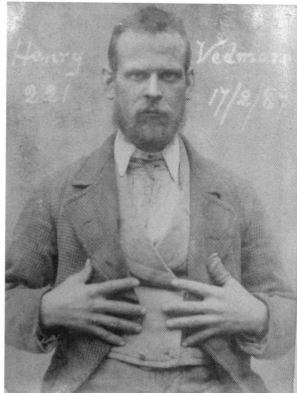

Charles Williford, 14 May 1870.   Henry Vedmore, 17 February 1887.

some have been torn and, particularly on the loose sheets, quite a few are dirty and even seem to have been trodden underfoot at some stage. Copying them using a digital camera has not been easy, due to reflecting light where the photographs do not lie flat and to the overlapping of pictures in the albums. It has been necessary to trim the resulting image to make them presentable. Occasionally the background has been adjusted but in no instance have the features of the prisoner been changed. They have been left as they were, warts and all!

The style of the photographs changed over the years. The earliest photographs, from 1870, were posed with the prisoner seated on a chair, with his or her hands placed in the lap, and giving as close up a picture as possible whilst not showing anything below the knees. The later photographs in this album showed a full length photograph of the prisoner, still mostly seated, which obviously gave less facial detail but more idea of the prisoner's overall size.

At the same time, very young children were snapped standing by the chair rather than seated on it. The photographs were not individually named but were attached to the relevant prisoner's record in the album.

As time progressed, just a portrait showing head and shoulders was used with the prisoner required to place his or her open hands on the waist or chest.

Arthur Stallard, 4 August 1894.

Thomas Bouton, 6 July 1906.

The name and number of the prisoner were chalked on the wall behind. As this style of photography was introduced before fingerprinting techniques were developed, it obviously gave the police and prison warders some indication of the size and shape of the hands if bloody or dirty handprints were left at the scene of the crime.

The next development was the use of an ingenious device which had a curved section removed from the bottom corner of a mirror. The prisoner was seated on a chair with the mirror placed over his right shoulder in such a way that the photograph when taken showed both full face and profile images at the same time. A board was attached to the wall behind for the recording of name, number and date.

The final innovation was the production of two separate images on one print, again one full face and one profile image. At this time, a wooden plank was placed in front of the prisoner and used to record name, number and date on the image.

The record shows that Charles Williford, filmed in May 1870, was a twenty-two-year-old labourer from Norton who was sentenced with, presumably, his brother Richard, aged twenty-five, to one month with hard labour for stealing a fowl. The gaol records for Henry Vedmore, Arthur Stallard and Thomas Bouten have not yet been found.

two

Clothes

Clothing worn by working class people is rarely shown in books on Victorian costumes so these photographs provide an interesting insight into what the worker, and more pertinently, the prisoner, wore on a normal day. In most cases, the prisoners wore whatever was provided for them by the prison system and their own clothes were discarded on arrival at the institution (and in Millbank Penitentiary at least, their clothes were sold cheaply to a dealer, so persistent offenders knew not to wear anything valuable when entering gaol!). However in some instances, the prisoners were obviously wearing their own apparel.

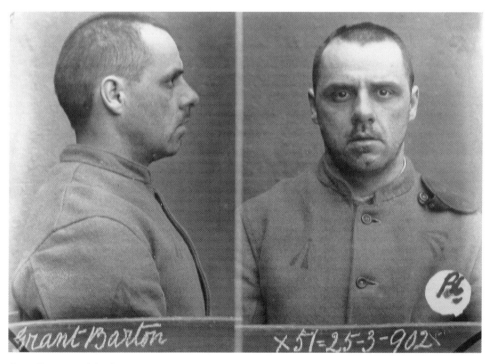

Grant Barton, 25 March 1902.

Charles Henry, 5 April 1906.

Harry Nelson, 8 January 1906.

 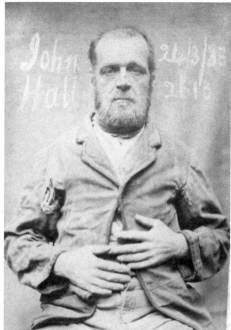

George Rea, 30 June 1884.   John Hall, 24 March 1883.

One of the early convicts can be seen wearing his prison outfit bearing the standard 'broad arrow' mark which indicated that the clothes were government property.

Some prisons used clothing of a particular combination of colours such as scarlet and grey or yellow and brown to identify their prisoners, but that does not appear to be the case for those photographed in Gloucester Gaol after 1870, although some of the prisoners using the treadmill were recorded in 1850 as being in a mixture of blue and yellow clothing. The outfits worn in these photographs were mainly dark and plain. And there were variations of clothing within the gaols to indicate the category of prisoner – whether, for instance, in the penitentiary or the debtors' prison or just on remand.

Standard uniform for male prisoners comprised boots, trousers, jacket, waistcoat, shirt and some sort of tie or neckerchief. A range of different shirts and neckwear can be seen in the following photographs. Underwear was unlikely to be provided until the twentieth century. Headgear seems to have been optional and a variety can be seen in the pictures from everyday working caps to bowler hats.

It looks as though there were suits of varying warmth, as some are made of thinner material, for summer use, whilst others are obviously more suited to the more severe cold weather of the winter months; whether or not prisoners were given a change of clothing as the seasons rotated is not known, though. Each prisoner, on arrival at the prison, was just handed the next suit of clothes available from the store, regardless of height or body shape. The condition and fit of the clothes was irrelevant, as can be seen in the photographs of George Rea and John Hall.

The following photographs show the variety of neckwear and headgear that was worn by male prisoners in the gaol. Hats and caps seem to have not been used in the later photographs.

The female prisoners appear to have been more likely to be wearing their own clothes. Although some were obviously in prison dress, others had a variety of clothing that presumably they wore when they entered the gaol.

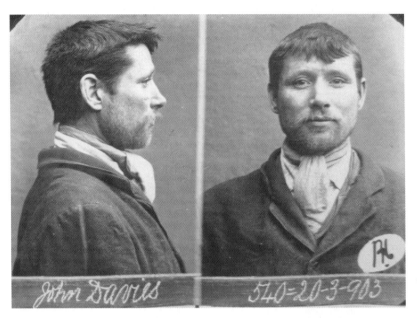

John Davies, 20 March 1903.

Thomas Surridge, 14 April 1896.

George Cole, 20 March 1903.

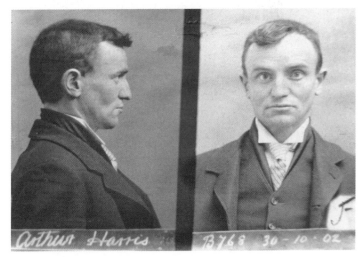

Arthur Harris (alias Bicknell), 30 October 1902.

John Coleman Pritchard, 28 July 1903.

John Harris, 7 December 1900.

Samuel Marston, 23 January 1903.

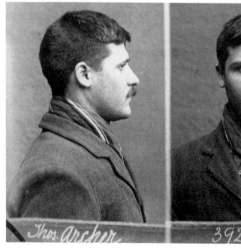

Thomas Archer, 21 January 1901.

William Mills,
8 November 1905.

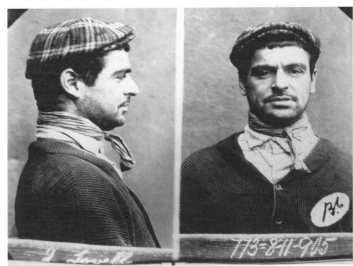

Joshua Lovell,
8 November 1905.

Albert Mytton, 5 March
1906.

William Nicholas,
4 December 1905.

George Jones, 6 July
1906.

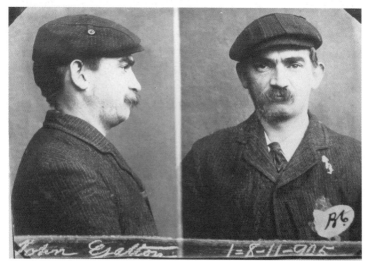

John Galton,
8 November 1905.

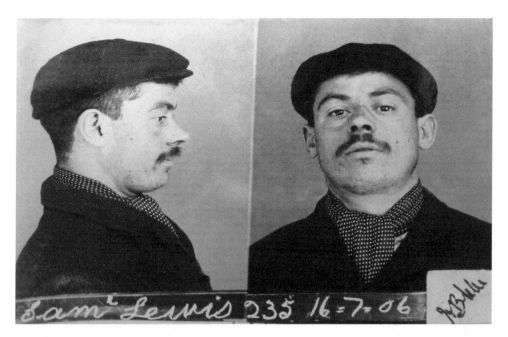

Samuel Lewis, 16 July 1906.

Emma Fountain, 18 June 1870.

Jane Harrison, 8 July 1886.

Finally, two of the convicts were soldiers still wearing their regimental uniforms. One was Joseph Burton, of whom no further details have been found. The other soldier photographed in his uniform was Frederick Taylor, born around 1882 in Drybrook, Gloucestershire, who is seen to be wearing the shoulder titles of the 3rd (Militia) Battalion of the Glosters, who were disbanded shortly after the end of the Boar War. His crime, for which he was sentenced to twelve months hard labour, was indecent assault.

Joseph Burton, 25 March 1902.

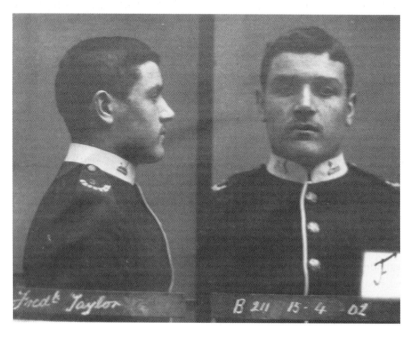

Frederick Taylor, 15 April 1902.

three

BOYS

In Victorian times, there was no distinction between children and adults when it came to a custodial sentence. In Lancashire, a child as young as three was known to have been sent to gaol alongside adults, but the youngest child photographed in Gloucester Gaol was imprisoned at the more advanced age of seven.

The age of majority at that time was twenty-one. Of the 1,045 prisoners recorded in the Gloucester Gaol albums, the ages of only 500 are known at present. Of these, 145, or more than 25 per cent, are under the age of twenty-one. This includes the seven-year-old and his nine-year-old brother, three other nine-year-olds, one ten-year-old, two eleven-year-olds and four twelve-year-olds; the latter included the youngest two girls. If we consider the current age of majority of eighteen years, then seventy-six children, or 15 per cent of those of known age, were held in the gaol.

The justice system seems to have been particularly hard on young offenders, presumably in an attempt to turn them away from a life of crime. Only one adult in the first album was given physical punishment as well as a custodial sentence but seven of the youngsters below the age of fourteen were whipped, getting anything up to twelve strokes with the birch rod, which, despite its gentle sounding nature, was a particularly unpleasant form of beating which frequently drew blood from the recipient.

The youngest prisoner held in Gloucester Gaol in 1870 was seven-year-old Edgar Leopold Kilminster who, together with his older brother Joseph William Kilminster, was sentenced to seven days with hard labour and to be given twelve strokes with the birch cane for the trivial offence of stealing sweetmeats. Imagine the feelings of those two small boys, taken from their family at such a tender age and incarcerated in the prison where separation or silence was the rule. Hopefully, at the very least, they were placed in the women's quarters.

Joseph and Edgar were the first two children of William Kilminster and his wife Harriett (née Gardiner) who went on to have a further seven children. The family lived in Chalford, near Bisley, where William worked as a cordwainer and where the children were born. When he was imprisoned, Edgar was described as having brown hair, grey eyes, a light complexion and a scar by his left eye. He was only 3ft 10in tall.

Clockwise from bottom left
Jesse Hooper, 18 June 1870.

Edgar Leopold Kilminster, the youngest prisoner
photographed, 25 June 1870.

William Joseph Kilminster, older brother of Edgar
Kilminster, 25 June 1870.

His brother, Joseph, although two years older, was actually one inch shorter and had brown hair, blue eyes, a fresh complexion and a hare lip. They were sentenced at Stroud Petty Sessions.

On 28 June 1870, the governor wrote in his journal:

Edgar and Joseph Kilminster, two boys, received 12 strokes each of a birch rod at 9 a.m.

Presumably their punishment was life changing, as they are not recorded in jail later on. They returned home to their parents and siblings and were found there in American Row, Chalford, on the 1881 census. Ten years later, Joseph had married, in 1887, to Louisa Paul and was living next door to his parents in 1891. By 1901, he had moved to Balsall Heath in Worcestershire where he was a boot-maker. Edgar also married, to Mary Griffin, but not until 1892. He was employed as a stick-maker.

Also sent to jail that year was nine-year-old Jesse Hooper. His crime was stealing a length of rope, for which he was sentenced to twenty days hard labour plus twelve strokes of the birch. He was described as being 4ft 2in tall, with light brown hair, grey eyes and a fresh complexion. He had obviously had an accident earlier in his childhood as he was recorded as having a 'burn scar on crown of head'. Sentenced at Gloucester City Petty Sessions on 30 May 1870, Jesse had no previous convictions.

On 1 June 1870, in his journal, the governor wrote:

Alfred Dix (or Dixon) and Jesse Hooper, two boys, received this morning, the former 9 strokes and the latter 12 strokes with a birch rod pursuant to sentences by the City Magistrates.

Jesse was born in Gloucester in 1860, the second son of Jesse Hooper senior and his wife Selina. The family lived at 67 Westgate Street, where the father was a marine store dealer, originally from Kidderminster. Jesse had followed his father into the local gaol. Jesse senior was remanded in custody there in November 1865 for deserting his family. His sentence is not known. When he grew up, young Jesse became a bill poster and married Harriet Maria Keene in 1883. No photograph has been found of Alfred Dix, but he was only eight years old when he was tried and sentenced in Gloucester for larceny.

An eleven-year-old boy held in Gloucester Gaol in 1870 was Charles Haines. Today, he would be above the age of criminal responsibility, which is currently ten years of age. He was born in Barnwood at the end of 1858 to George Haines and Lydia (née Waite), who had married in Kings Stanley earlier that year. Young Charles was the oldest of their six known children and was sentenced to twenty-one days with hard labour plus twelve strokes of the birch for stealing money. He was described at the time as being 4ft 7in tall, with brown hair, dark grey eyes and a light complexion.

Henry Smith, also born in Barnwood, was twelve years old when he was sentenced to five days hard labour and nine strokes of the birch rod for stealing money. He had light coloured hair, dark grey eyes and a fresh complexion.

Charles Haines, 4 June 1870.

Henry Smith, 21 May 1870.

Above, left and right Alfred Taylor, the last entry in
the first album, was fourteen years old when he was
sentenced to ten days hard labour for the crime
of stealing two chickens and some tame rabbits at
Bitton. Also charged alongside him was eighteen-
year-old Samuel Taylor, his brother. They are believed
to be the children of Isaac Taylor, a collier, and his
wife Sarah. Born in Thornbury around 1856, Alfred,
in 1870, was 4ft 10in tall, had dark brown hair, brown
eyes and a fresh complexion, with a mole on his
neck and between his shoulders. His occupation was
given as labourer. Samuel was 5ft 8in tall, with dark
hair, dark brown eyes and a dark complexion. Their
likeness is evident from the photographs.

Right Walter Bond, aged sixteen, was sentenced to
three months of hard labour for stealing fowls. He
was 5ft 3in tall, had brown hair, grey eyes and a fresh
complexion. He also had two moles on his left arm
and a scar on his right knee. Walter was one of three
sons of John and Elizabeth Bond who lived at
5 Buckle's Row in Charlton Kings when he was
young.

Above, left and right James Hucker, a labourer, and
Charles Mills, a shoemaker, both seventeen years
of age, were convicted together of stealing four
ducks and a drake at Horfield. James originated
in Somerset and Charles in Bristol. Both youths
were sentenced to six months of hard labour and
five years under police supervision, their sentences
reflecting the fact that they both had previous
convictions. Charles, at 5ft 2in, had light brown hair,
hazel eyes and a sallow, pock-marked complexion.
He had previous convictions, one for stealing
potatoes, for which he served a fortnight with hard
labour and one for stealing tools; for this crime,
the length of sentence was increased to six weeks.
James was slightly taller than Charles, with brown
hair, grey hazel eyes and a fresh complexion. His
distinguishing marks all appear to have been tattoos,
with an image of a sailor and the initials JH on his
left arm, four dots on his left hand and a bracelet on
his right wrist. Like Charles, he had two previous
convictions; the first was for stealing thirty-five pairs
of socks for which he served twenty days with hard
labour; the second offence, committed in February
1869, was stealing a coat for which he received a
three-month sentence with hard labour.

Sidney Alfred Lasbury was born in 1887 in the Stroud area. In 1904, at the age of seventeen, he was found guilty of stealing 24s, and sentenced to two months of hard labour. He was the son of Walter Lasbury and his wife Emily, formerly Nicholls. In 1901, the family were living in Horns Road in Stroud.

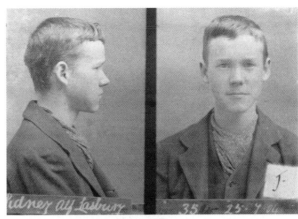

David Hyam was a seventeen-year-old from Gloucester when he was gaoled for six weeks with hard labour in 1902. His crime had been housebreaking and stealing therein one gold ring, one knife, etc. He was a labourer and claimed to be a member of the Church of England.

Alfred Horatius (or Horatio) Tennant was also seventeen in 1902. He was born in Reading and was working as a draper's assistant when he fell foul of the law. His crime was stealing a bicycle and, when he was found guilty, he was given a sentence of four weeks with hard labour. He professed to be a member of the Wesleyan faith.

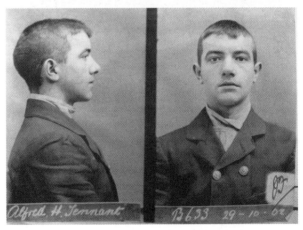

Opposite The birth place of David O'Brien, at some time around 1853, is not clear. One record has it as being in Buckinghamshire whilst another claims it was in Berkshire. He was actually sentenced at Stroud Petty Sessions and it was there that he planned to return on his release. He had brown hair and eyes, a fresh complexion and DD on his right arm. One wonders whether that was a misreading of DO or whether it was indicative of an alias.

Arthur Henry Jones was photographed in Gloucester Gaol in March 1902. He was sentenced to six calendar months with hard labour followed by one year under police supervision for stealing a bicycle. Arthur was an eighteen-year-old collier, born in Bristol and a member of the Church of England.

Also eighteen years old in 1902 was Albert Payton, a labourer who had been imprisoned for six weeks with hard labour for shop-breaking and stealing therein £1 12s 1d. Albert came from Cheltenham and was a member of the Church of England.

In May 1904, Frederick Saroney, aged 18, was photographed in gaol whilst serving two months with hard labour for house breaking. A labourer from Cheltenham, Frederick gave his religion as being Church of England.

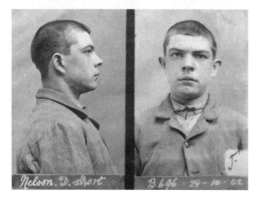

Nelson Daniel Short was eighteen when he was imprisoned for stealing £1 in money. A gardener born in Cheltenham, Nelson was given a sentence of one calendar month plus hard labour for his crime. He gave his religion as being Church of England.

William Henry Williams came from Kidderminster. Born about 1883, he was imprisoned in 1901 for stealing £2 10s, the money belonging to Abraham Matthews. William, a striker (a blacksmith's assistant), was sentenced to one calendar month with hard labour. When asked, William said he belonged to the Church of England.

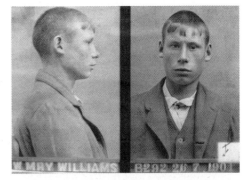

Walter James Wood was another eighteen-year-old held in Gloucester Gaol. A labourer, born around 1886 in Cheltenham, Walter was jailed for housebreaking. His sentence was for three calendar months with hard labour. Walter also gave his religion as being Church of England.

All that is known about eighteen-year-old blacksmith Thomas Tomming, who occasionally used the alias Henry Philips, is that he originated in Birmingham and was found guilty of stealing money for which he was sentenced to six weeks of hard labour. On his release, he intended to return to his home town.

Above and right There were three young men called John Smith imprisoned in Gloucester Gaol, as well as an older man of the same name. The first John Smith was an eighteen-year-old wheelwright who came from Leckhampton and who was found guilty of burglary in 1870, for which he was sentenced to six months of hard labour. He was charged with breaking and entering a house in Cheltenham where he stole five bracelets, one charm, a brooch, a knife and a cucumber! One of the taller youngsters in gaol, at 5ft 7in, John had brown hair, grey eyes and a fresh complexion. Many years later, in 1902, another eighteen-year-old John Smith, this time a labourer from Cheltenham, was sentenced to six weeks of hard labour for shop-breaking and stealing £1 12s 1d. The third John Smith was photographed twice, in 1892 and 1893. No further details of him have been found yet.

Clockwise from above Russell Botchett was sixteen when he was gaoled in 1902. Russell was born in Hereford at the end of 1886, the son of a shoemaker, Charles Botchett and his wife Lucy. Details of the crime for which Russell was sentenced are not known.

Another sixteen-year-old from outside of Gloucestershire imprisoned in the same year was John Bartlett Morrish. He came from Little Weston in Somerset where he was a farmer's assistant. His crime was stealing £12 for which he was given a four-calendar-month sentence with hard labour.

Alfred Smith was nineteen when he was sent to Gloucester Gaol in 1870 for the offence of stealing wearing apparel. Before he went into prison, Alfred was a sail-maker. He was sentenced to six weeks of hard labour for his crime and, although born in Gloucester, he said that he planned to go to Swindon, in Wiltshire, on his release.

Opposite below, from far left Henry Gardner, a nineteen-year-old from Tredworth, in Gloucester, was found guilty of housebreaking and sentenced to two months of hard labour. He was described as a striker, an assistant to a blacksmith.

Benjamin Hathaway was born in the first quarter of 1850 in the St Martin's district of London. In 1870, aged nineteen, he found himself charged with stealing a £10 bank note, was found guilty and sentenced to six months with hard labour followed by seven years under police supervision. On his release, he planned to stay in Cheltenham where his parents, William and Maria Hathaway lived. Benjamin had a previous conviction for malicious damage.

William Longstreet, an eighteen-year-old labourer from Berkeley, was charged with cheating and obtaining goods by false pretences. He was 5ft 2in tall, had brown hair and blue eyes. The full record of his crime accused him of obtaining by false pretences 6 yards of linsey (sic), a leather belt and 12 yards of flannel and also of stealing one coat and a pair of shoes, one loaf of bread, 2lb of biscuits, 6lb sugar, 1lb of tea and ½ of tobacco, to which he pleaded guilty. William was the second child and eldest son of the eight children born to Daniel Longstreet, a farm labourer, and his wife Ann from Berkeley Heath. He was a member of the Independent religion and was one of the few young prisoners who could read properly; most had received a limited education. In court, he was sentenced to six months of hard labour.

First row, left to right According to his record, Percy Jobbins was born in Stratton in Wiltshire around 1884 and had signed up to be a soldier. But at some stage of his army career he committed the crime of 'burglariously breaking into a dwelling house and therein stealing one clock'. For his crime, Percy was sentenced to six months gaol with hard labour. He claimed that his religion was Church of England.

Lionel Vivian Holder was a local boy who was employed as a clerk. But towards the end of 1902 he was found guilty of stealing £7 10s and given a sentence of one calendar month in gaol. Lionel stated that his religion was Church of England.

John Morgan was a collier from Lydbrook in the Forest of Dean. It is quite likely that he was one of the many Morgans who were free-miners there. Aged nineteen in 1901, he was sentenced to three months with hard labour for housebreaking. John was a member of the Church of England.

Second row, left to right Herbert Stanley was nineteen years old when he was jailed in 1901. Herbert originated in Overbury in Worcestershire and was a member of the Church of England. His crime was stealing a bicycle for which he was given a sentence of one calendar month with hard labour.

Another nineteen-year-old was Albert Walker. Born in Wolverhampton around 1883, Albert was a labourer who occasionally used the alias of Albert Brooks. He was found guilty of stealing 9s 6d, a silver watch and chain, one trinket and a gold ring, amongst other items. For this he was sentenced to two months in gaol with hard labour. Albert stated that his religion was Church of England.

Stephen Wilcox was a tailor charged with stealing a bicycle and given four calendar months in gaol with hard labour. A member of the Church of England, Stephen was born around 1884 but his birth place was not recorded.

Opposite, left In 1870, George Coleman, a twenty-year-old labourer from Herefordshire, was sentenced to one month of hard labour for stealing a rabbit trap. George was the fourth of six children born to John and Ann Coleman of Aston Ingham, just outside the Gloucestershire border. His mother died when he was a child. George stated that he intended to go to Newent on his release.

Opposite, right Charles Dee, aged twenty from Avening, was the only married minor in the album. Born in Avening, the son of Robert Dee, a stone sawyer, and his wife, Harriet, a woollen cloth worker, he was one of eight children. In 1870, Charles was a labourer when he was apprehended in Rodborough, charged with stealing an axe, found guilty of the crime and sentenced to twelve months with hard labour. This was one of his three appearances at court.

Above, from left William Barker was a twenty-year-old sailor who found his way to the county of Gloucestershire in 1904 where he was found guilty of burglary and office breaking. William, who originated in Oldham around 1884 and claimed to be a member of the Church of England, was given a four-month sentence in gaol with hard labour.

Unlike most of the prisoners, Reginald Joseph Grundy stated that his faith was that of the Primitive Methodists. Born in Hereford around 1884, Reginald was a carpenter who was accused of sheep stealing. When found guilty, he was sentenced to one month in Gloucester Gaol with hard labour.

James Morgan was twenty years old in 1903 when his photograph was taken in Gloucester Gaol. Originating in Hoxton in London, James was a joiner by trade. He stole a silver watch 'from the person' – obviously a pickpocket. He appears to have been a long term offender, occasionally using the alias of Charles Fenley and was therefore given a more serious sentence of five years of penal servitude which would either have been served in the penitentiary section of the local gaol or he would have been sent to another centre, such as Pentonville Prison.

There are eight photographs of prisoners who were obviously young, but for which there is no available information other than the name and date on the photograph itself. They are:

Thomas Clarke, 30 June 1898.

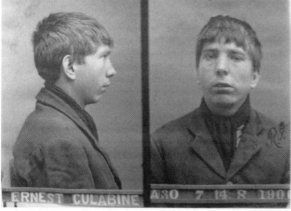

Ernest Culabine, 14 August 1900.

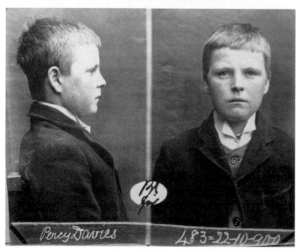

Percy Davies, 22 October 1900.

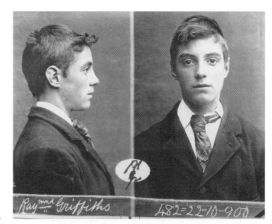

Raymond Griffiths, 22 October 1900.

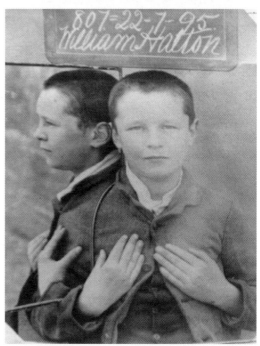

William Hatton, 22 July 1895.

David Powell, 20 June 1898.

John Henry Williams, 19 July 1888.

Thomas Stephens, 16 October 1888.

four

GIRLS

There were far fewer girls held in Gloucester Gaol than boys. Of the 282 prisoners listed in the first album, only seventy-one, just over a quarter of them, were female, with ages ranging from twelve to fifty-five years old, although a later album showed an older woman of sixty-two in the gaol. The early albums have only eight photographs of girls, each showing a fairly standard uniform of long dress, apron and cape. It also looks as though it was the norm for hair to be parted down the middle and pulled back into a bun of some kind.

The youngest girls entered in the 'Return of Habitual Criminals' of 1870 were two twelve-year-olds, Sarah Jordan and Sarah Morgan, for whom no photographs were included. Sarah Jordan was a servant from Cheltenham, described as being 4ft 10in tall, with brown hair, hazel eyes and a fine complexion. She also had a scar under her right eye and several moles on her left arm. She was charged with obtaining by false pretences one pan of broth with intent to defraud at Cheltenham on 26 November 1869. She was found guilty of cheating and sentenced to six weeks of hard labour in gaol and five years at the Red Lodge Reformatory School, which was in Park Road in Bristol. Her father was said to live at 2 Suffolk Street, Bath Road in Cheltenham, but no more details were given for him. Sarah was described in gaol as being of 'indifferent character'.

Sarah Morgan originated from Wallingford in Oxfordshire. She was recorded as being a tramp and there is no evidence that she was accompanied on the road by others — travelling alone would have been a frightening situation for a twelve-year-old to find herself in. Her crime, for which she was sentenced to ten days of hard labour, was stealing shirts.

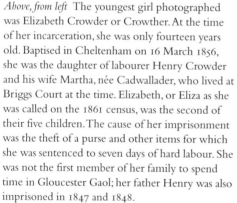

Above, from left The youngest girl photographed
was Elizabeth Crowder or Crowther. At the time
of her incarceration, she was only fourteen years
old. Baptised in Cheltenham on 16 March 1856,
she was the daughter of labourer Henry Crowder
and his wife Martha, née Cadwallader, who lived at
Briggs Court at the time. Elizabeth, or Eliza as she
was called on the 1861 census, was the second of
their five children. The cause of her imprisonment
was the theft of a purse and other items for which
she was sentenced to seven days of hard labour. She
was not the first member of her family to spend
time in Gloucester Gaol; her father Henry was also
imprisoned in 1847 and 1848.

The next youngest girl to have her photograph
taken was Ellen Wood. At fifteen years of age, she
was sentenced to one month of hard labour for
stealing postage stamps. A servant from Newnham,
she planned to return to the Forest of Dean after
her release.

Above left Maria Lane was a seventeen-year-old servant, 5ft 2in tall with fair hair, blue eyes and a ruddy complexion. The thorough physical examination on entry to the gaol also revealed a wart on her right elbow. She was charged with stealing gloves and other items, found guilty of larceny and sentenced to one month with hard labour in the gaol. The record stated that her ability to read and write was limited. Maria was the oldest of four children born to Charles Lane and his wife, Ann, née Lyddiat, who married in St Mary de Lode church in Gloucester in 1853. When Maria was released from gaol, she returned to her family home at 5 High Orchard Street in Gloucester.

Above right Another seventeen-year-old held in the gaol was Catherine Ann Mott. She was charged with stealing meat, found guilty and sentenced to two months of hard labour. Catherine, a charwoman, is believed to be the third child of seven born to William and Jane Mott, but she was usually known just as Ann. William married Jane Webb at Cheltenham Register Office in 1846. On her release from gaol, Catherine returned to her family in Cheltenham

Opposite A year older than Ellen was Kate Wheeler who originated from Leamington in Warwickshire. She was described in the register as being 5ft 2in tall, with dark brown hair and grey eyes and a burn scar on her left knee. Kate was unemployed when she committed the crime of stealing a blanket and obtaining 8 yards of calico by false pretences with intent to defraud, for which offence she received a sentence of three months of hard labour. Obviously, this was the start of a slippery slope for Kate as, five years later, she was back in gaol, this time described as a prostitute.

Above, left and centre Emma Hawkins was charged, with her older sister Elizabeth, with stealing coal. Both girls worked as charwomen. This was their second offence – presumably the family were unable to purchase enough coal to keep themselves warm. She was sentenced for her crime at Coleford Petty Sessions to six weeks with hard labour. Emma was seventeen at the time, 4ft 10in tall with brown hair, grey eyes and a fair complexion. She was born at Lydbrook in the Forest of Dean, the fourth child of the seven born to coalminer Thomas Hawkins and Emily, née Bozley, whom he married in 1844 in St Briavels. Emma was described as having a 'full neck, a mole near her left eye and on her left cheek'. Her sister, Elizabeth, was described as 4ft 8in tall, with dark brown hair, dark blue eyes and a sallow complexion. Unusually, a note was added to the bottom of Elizabeth's record which stated, 'this prisoner is considered a very suspicious character'!

Above, right Emma Dyke was nineteen years old when she was arrested for stealing money. The record described her as being 5ft 6in tall, with dark brown hair, brown eyes, a florid complexion and large features. It also said she was a prostitute, though a second record said she was unemployed at the time. She was charged with stealing 4s from one Edward Forrester in North Hamlet and pleaded guilty to larceny, for which she was sentenced to six months of hard labour and seven years under police supervision. The severity of this sentence reflected the fact that she had more then one previous conviction, for stealing and drunkenness. Her mother was listed as Caroline Dyke of 15 Grove Street, Cheltenham. As no father's name was given, it is assumed that Emma was illegitimate. When Emma left gaol, she found a job working as a domestic servant for John Hill, the landlord of the Suffolk Arms in Cheltenham.

Sarah Britton was the oldest of the girls photographed for the Return of Habitual Criminals. She was twenty years old in 1870 when she was charged with stealing a watch. Found guilty, she was sentenced to three months of hard labour. Sarah originated from Hanham in the south of Gloucestershire and worked as a servant. On her release, she was planning to return to Bristol.

five

ELDERLY PRISONERS

The oldest prisoner held in Gloucester Gaol was William Lord, who was seventy-nine years old when he was remanded on 1 October 1869. William was born in Ashbury in Berkshire on 2 September 1790 and baptised there three days later. He was the second known son of William Lord senior and his wife Mary Wellovise, who were married in the parish in 1787. At some point, William moved to Kempsford on the Gloucestershire border and there he married Hannah Edwards in 1815 and had several children, although his final gaol record recorded him as single – this could have been because he had been widowed for over twenty years.

He was described as being only 5ft 2in tall, with grey hair, grey eyes and a fresh complexion. He also had a cut left wrist and his second finger on his right hand was contracted.

William Lord, the oldest prisoner photographed, on 11 June 1870.

William was charged with stealing a quantity of timber at Kempsford and found guilty of larceny. For this he was sentenced to six months of hard labour and seven years of police supervision thereafter, the severity of the sentence reflecting his previous convictions. His record stated that he had been 'known to PC Bowly for twenty years' and had been in the gaol for stealing before. But William did not complete his six-month sentence. His health was obviously giving cause for concern as the chaplain regularly recorded in his journal that he had visited the sick, one of whom was William Lord. Eventually, on 9 June 1870, the governor wrote in his journal:

Her Majesty's pardon for William Lord received – who is discharged.

A note on his record states that:

William Lord was removed to his home in charge of Hospital Warder Mr Clutterbuck.

Sadly, his ill health continued and William died before the end of September 1870.

At sixty years of age, in 1902 Harry Radford found himself in Gloucester Gaol, sentenced to two months with hard labour for stealing a pair of boots. Harry was an oil refiner and, as a photograph appeared of him in the earlier album, was obviously a repeat offender. In fact, a search of the gaol's Register of Previous Convictions demonstrated just how much of a repeat offender he actually was. It is interesting to note how far Harry travelled around the country during his criminal career. The record shows his convictions as:

Year	Location	Crime	Sentence	Alias Used
1901	Marylebone	Stealing an overcoat	7 weeks	Thomas Murphy
1902	Cheltenham	Stealing boots	2 months	
1903	Plymouth	Stealing an overcoat	6 months	Henry Williams
1906	Hereford	False Pretences	2 months	Richard Bird
1907	Salisbury	False Pretences	6 months	
1908	Bath	False Pretences	1 month	
1908	Gloucester	Stealing a child's cradle	1 day	

As well as these listed convictions, Harry had fifteen summary convictions for drunkenness and begging between 1908 and the end of 1912, these last offences being mainly within the county of Gloucestershire. Perhaps the clue to Harry's lifestyle is disclosed in the note in the file:

Removed to Gloucester County Lunatic Asylum by order of the Secretary of State, 10th June 1908. Prisoner having been removed to Lunatic Asylum, trial postponed to these Sessions. Certified sane and received into prison by the Secretary of State's order on 15th October 1908.

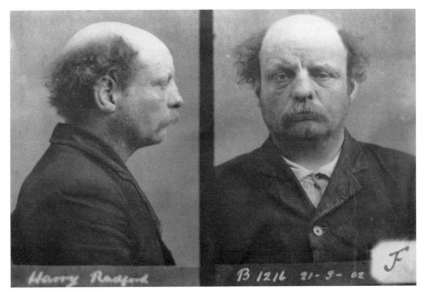

Harry Radford, 21 March 1902.

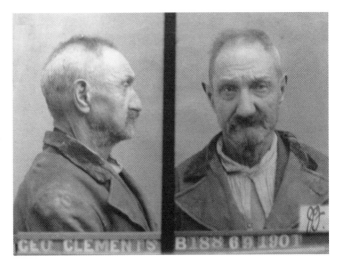

The second oldest prisoner recorded in Gloucester Gaol was George Clements who, also aged seventy-nine, was in prison in 1901 serving a three-month sentence, with hard labour, for stealing food and clothing from a vessel. George was a boatman by trade and gave his place of birth as Arlingham. He also stated that he was a member of the Church of England.

Two other elderly prisoners were Thomas Williams and Edward Thompson. Thomas Williams was sixty-six when held in Gloucester Gaol in 1870 but no photograph was taken of him. Born in Cheltenham around 1804, Thomas intended to go to Birmingham when he was released. A shoemaker by trade, his crime was stealing boots and for that he was sentenced to one year of hard labour.

Edward Thompson was sixty-three years old when his photograph was taken on 24 April 1899. Born in Bristol around 1836, Edward was a tailor and member of the Church of England who was sentenced to eighteen months in prison with hard labour. His crime was stealing a purse and 5s 7d 'from the person'. Although a photograph still exists for Edward, it is of very poor quality and therefore is not used here.

  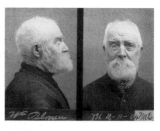

Above, from left Daniel Henry Kinsey, a seventy-seven year old from Leominster, was photographed in the gaol on 3 February 1904. Daniel, a member of the Congregationalist Church, was a builder who was found guilty of stealing one silver paten and one silver box. For this, he was sentenced to twelve months with hard labour and, afterwards, five years under police supervision.

Richard Edwards was, at seventy-five years of age, one of the oldest prisoners to be held in Gloucester Gaol in 1902. His crime was a serious one of shooting with intent. He was found guilty of grievous bodily harm and sentenced to eleven months gaol with hard labour. A butcher, born in Bisley, Richard claimed to be a member of the Church of England.

William Palmer was held twice in Gloucester Gaol in 1904, first in January for stealing one flask basket and one hammer, for which he was given a two-month sentence with hard labour. Before his next visit, William celebrated his seventy-second birthday. On 14 November 1904, he was photographed again. His crime this time was lodging in an outhouse and he was given three months. William was a boatman and was born in Berkeley around 1832.

Below, from left Richard Walford was sixty years old when he was sentenced to ten days with hard labour in Gloucester Gaol for the then crime of attempting suicide. What brought him to perform such a drastic act? Richard was born in Lydbrook in 1841 to coalminer William Walford and his wife Eliza. As he grew up, Richard began work in the local iron works and in 1870 he married Charlotte Probert. Seven children were born to the couple over the years and by the 1890s Richard was working as a coal dealer. He was said to be a dissenter rather than a member of the Church of England.

Sixty-two-year-old George Bridges was another sad case. He was sentenced to ten days of hard labour in 1901 for having attempted to commit suicide. George was a plasterer born in Painswick who gave his religion as being Church of England.

John Clare was also sixty-two years of age when he was photographed in Gloucester Gaol on 23 May 1902. John was a carpenter by trade and was given a one-month sentence with hard labour for stealing carpenter's tools. John gave Huntingdon as his place of birth and Church of England as his religion. Occasionally he used the alias Samuel Saint.

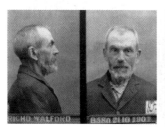 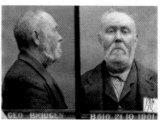 

John Edwards, also known as John Craig, was born around 1804, so was sixty-six years old when he was imprisoned. His crime was one of burglary and for that he was given a sentence of three months with hard labour. John was said to be a single man and his occupation was given as clerk/tramp so presumably he had been a clerk in better days, but in 1870 was out of work and travelling in the hope of finding a job. His birth place was recorded as being Chester and he planned to go to Liverpool on his release.

Below, from left William Curtis was born around 1840, according to his prison record, in Ledworth in Wiltshire, although this has not been confirmed. His crime, in 1902, was to steal ten half crowns and for this he was sentenced to twenty-one days in gaol with hard labour. William had not decided where he would go once he had completed his sentence. A labourer, William stated that he was a member of the congregation of the Church of England.

John Gwynn, born around 1842 in London, was sixty years of age when he was imprisoned in Gloucester Gaol in 1902. John, a printer by trade and a member of the Church of England, had stolen 7s and 6d and was sentence to eighteen months in prison with hard labour for his sins.

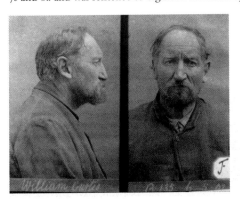
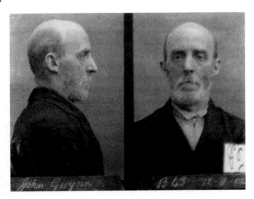

Others who, from their pictures appear to be elderly, but for whom no details have been located, are:

Joseph Davis, 2 September 1902.

William Jones, 5 February 1900.

Left John Hade, 27 May 1890.

Right Thomas Harris, 18 January 1892.

Left Thomas Ward, 30 June 1894.

Right James Burton, 4 April 1887.

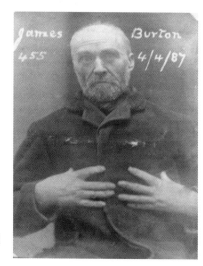

Top row, from left
Frederick Halson, 5 May 1905.

Alexander Kelly, 4 July 1903.

Alfred Mason, 19 August 1904.

Second row
Henry Titch, 16 September 1904.

Thomas Johns, 8 November 1905.

Third row
John Jones, 6 July 1906.

William Mason, 15 June 1899.

James Slack, 15 June 1899.

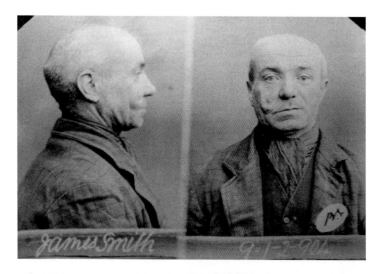

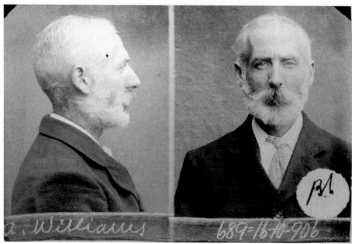

Clockwise from left
James Williams, 8 March 1894.

Alfred Williams, 16 October 1906.

James Smith, 1 February 1904.

six

WOMEN PRISONERS

Women were in the minority in Gloucester Gaol in the nineteenth century. There were 128 females included in the Gloucester Gaol albums compared with 917 men and boys, approximately 12 per cent of the total number of prisoners mentioned. As there were many other prisoners in gaol besides those in the albums, it is impossible to know how accurately this reflects the general prison population at the time.

Most of the women imprisoned in the gaol were those recorded in the first album and very few of them had photographs. Of the later female prisoners, less information has been found either on their crimes or their circumstances. The women had their own separate section of the prison but, eventually, all female prisoners were removed from Gloucester Gaol when it was utilised by the Prison Commissioners as an additional facility for holding male convicts under sentence of penal servitude.

Mary Shield was just twenty-one and unemployed when in May 1870 she was arrested for stealing 'a slop', which could have been one of several different items of wearing apparel. Originating in Birmingham, Mary was recorded as being a tramp. Once she had served her sentence of fourteen days in gaol with hard labour, she planned to head for the town of Cheltenham.

Above, from left Another woman recorded as being a tramp was Harriet Hancock Wyatt, who originated from Southampton. A single woman aged twenty-three, Harriet was sentenced to one month with hard labour when she was convicted in 1870 of cheating. Her intention on leaving gaol was to go to Lower Norwood.

Frances Darnell was a Roman Catholic woman who had travelled across the country from her birth place in Lincolnshire. In 1904, when she was arrested along with James Darnell, presumably a spouse or sibling, Frances was twenty-five years old and unemployed. Her crime was one of burglary and the stealing of two sheets. For this she was given one of the longer sentences for a woman in the albums – that of nine months with hard labour. She did not know where she was going when she was released.

Elizabeth Hill was forty-two years old when she was sentenced for the crime of stealing bed linen in 1870. Married and working as a charwoman in Cheltenham, Elizabeth was given a sentence of two months in gaol, with hard labour, followed by two years under police supervision.

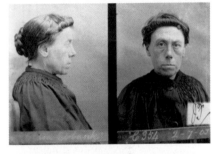

Clara Ewbank was one of the older female prisoners at the age of fifty-one. She was born in Scotland around 1852 and she gave her occupation as that of nurse. Her crime, in 1903, was rather unusual – endeavouring to procure charitable contributions by false pretences. When she was found guilty, she was sentenced to fourteen days with hard labour. A member of the Church of Scotland, Clara sometimes used the alias of Emily McKay.

Alice Foley was a twenty-five-year-old woman from Cardiff who was working as a prostitute when she was arrested just after Christmas in 1902 on charges of obtaining money by false pretences, and was imprisoned awaiting trial. However, when her case came up in court, she was discharged. Alice was a member of the Church of England.

Opposite, from far left Jane Norton was a washer woman, aged twenty-seven, when she was photographed in gaol in May 1870. Her crime was stealing a tablecloth for which she was sentenced to three months with hard labour. Although she was born in Lechlade, on her release she intended to remain in the city of Gloucester.

Sarah Ann Bailey stated that she was born in Hasfield (possibly Haresfield?) but intended to go to Harescombe when she had served her time. Sarah was aged thirty-nine, married and unemployed in 1870 when she was arrested and charged with stealing 'dress stuff'. Found guilty, Sarah was sentenced to one month of hard labour in the gaol.

Born in Gloucester around 1850, Eliza Ann Jones was probably the oldest women held in the gaol and recorded in the photograph albums in 1902. Eliza was a laundress found guilty of stealing a skirt for which she was sentenced to six calendar months with hard labour. She was recorded as being a member of the Church of England.

Mary Jane Oland was born in Kempsford thirty years before she had to pose for her photograph in Gloucester Gaol. Her occupation, in 1902, was that of a needlewoman and she claimed to be a member of the Church of England. She was charged with burglary and given a relatively long sentence of twelve months with hard labour. At some point during her incarceration, she was transferred to Ipswich Prison.

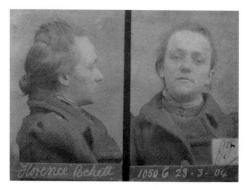

Florence Pockett was one of the few women prisoners who was photographed more than once. The first photograph was dated 10 July 1901 and the second one was taken nearly three years later on 23 March 1904. Born in Manchester around 1871, Florence had no occupation when arrested. Her first recorded offence was stealing a child's mail cart for which she was given six weeks with hard labour. For her second offence of larceny, she was given a longer sentence, this time of three months plus hard labour. Florence stated that her religion was that of the Church of England.

Alice Puffett was twenty-three years old and a member of the Church of England when she was photographed in gaol in November 1901. Born in Filkins, on the Oxfordshire/Gloucestershire border, she worked as a servant. Found guilty of obtaining wearing apparel by false pretences, Alice was sentenced to six weeks with hard labour.

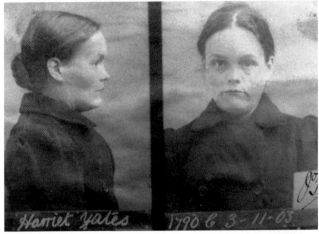

Above, from left Mary O'Ryan was born in Southsea around 1834 but was found guilty of cheating in 1870 and sentenced to one month with hard labour in Gloucester Gaol. Mary was a tramp and a married woman. On her release, she intended to go to Brompton.

Harriet Yates originated from Newent having been born there around 1873. She was aged thirty and unemployed when she was arrested late in 1903, charged with stealing boots and sentenced to one calendar month of hard labour. Harriet professed to be a member of the Baptist Church.

Elizabeth Milton, aged thirty-eight in 1901, was born in Cardiff. The record does not state whether she was married or single but gives her occupation as a charwoman. Elizabeth, a member of the Church of England, was found guilty of stealing three pairs of trousers and sentenced to one month in gaol with hard labour.

Annie Brown was recorded as being a prostitute, born in Cheltenham. She was twenty-eight years old and a member of the Church of England when she was photographed in November 1901. Her crime was one of stealing 2*s* and 6*d*, for which she was given five months with hard labour.

There are fifty-five female prisoners for whom information is available but no photographs. Most of these were recorded in the 'Return of Habitual Criminals' dated 1870, but some appear at a later date.

The following female prisoners were photographed but few details of them or their crimes have been found.

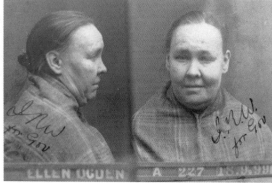

From far left
Ann Glover,
13 October
1882.

Ellen Ogden,
18 September
1899.

Mary Ward, 11 December 1899.   Kate Brown, 30 August 1899.

From right
Julia Brown,
26 July 1900.

Harriet
Agnes
Chappel,
18 July 1888.

Lucy Clarke, 26 July 1897.

Mary Coffee, 18 February 1893.

Sarah Ann Cooke, 16 July 1889.

Elizabeth Davies, 3 March 1903.

Harriet Jarvis, 27 July 1887.

Florence Kennedy (alias Davis), 29 December 1887.

Ellen Lancaster, 27 June 1884.

Top row, from left Mary Ann Lee (alias Garrity), 5 July 1883.

Margaret Martin, 1 July 1895.

Martha Mason, 15 April 1886, 4 November 1890, 1 July 1895.

Second row Catherine McKenna, 29 September 1888.

Mary Ann Payne (alias Jarvis and Freeman), 29 June 1883.

Susan Price, 23 March 1895.

Third row Theresa Pritchard, 28 January 1886.

Emily Ridley, 21 April 1890.

Left Sarah Ann Roberts 17 March 1905.

Clockwise from above, left
Rose Weeks, 1 November 1900.

Jane Barrett (alias Sullivan), 18 December 1902.

Susan Ryan, 27 October 1888.

Maria Simmons, (alias Annie Holloway), 29 December 1887. Transferred from Birmingham.

Sarah Ann Storey (alias Berry), 17 March 1905.

Emily Watts, 27 March 1886.

Rose White, 30 April 1901.

Anti-clockwise, from left
Cath Wilson, 1 November 1900.

Susannah Formby, 9 July 1885.

Elizabeth Chandler, 1 October 1883 and 4 October 1884.

Elizabeth Taylor, 3 November 1890, 25 March 1893 and 20 September 1898.

Mary Ann Williams, 9 January 1885.

Mary Ann Whittaker, 7 January 1884.

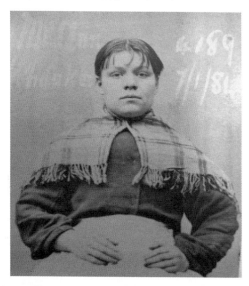

seven

FAMILY GROUPS

Does crime run in families? This was obviously the case for the Wilson trio who were held in Gloucester Gaol in 1870. Three of them, probably a man, his wife and his sister, from Plymouth, were classified as tramps with an uncertain destination on release. Walter Wilson was twenty-four years old, married and a shoemaker before he took to the road. Elizabeth, aged twenty-one, was the middle of the three and also married; Emma Wilson, the youngest of the three at nineteen years old, was named as a prostitute. Their crime was stealing wearing apparel and they were each sentenced to six months with hard labour.

It is not so easy to tell whether any of the other prisoners held in Gloucester Gaol were actually related to any of the others, particularly those called Smith or Jones, but with one or two of the more unusual names it seems obvious that there must be some connection. Take, for instance, the surname of Castree; it occurs nine times in the photograph albums between 1883 and 1894 and at least seven of these are clearly separate individuals, either from their forenames or from their physical appearance.

The Castree family appear in the albums where no additional details are available. Some of the family seem to have originated in the Garway and Orcop areas of Herefordshire and can be found there during the censuses of 1871 and 1881. From his photograph, Charles Castree is obviously the oldest amongst the group and Jeremiah Castree would appear to be the youngest. The 1871 census has a Charles Castree, aged forty-four, living at Stone Wall in Garway with a son Jeremiah, aged four. The latter could well be the strapping lad photographed in 1884, but the Charles photographed in 1885 is looking rather older than the fifty-eight years that he would be if this is indeed Jeremiah's father.

Other Castree prisoners were David, Edwin, George, James and William. David sometimes used the alias

Charles Castree, 30 June 1885.

Left David Castree,
21 July 1886.

Right Edwin Castree,
30 June 1894.

Left George Castree,
1 July 1884 and
2 April 1887.

Right James Castree,
15 October 1883 and
26 August 1889.

Left Jeremiah Castree,
30 September 1884.

Right William
Castree, 27 February
1889.

of George Powell. Some of these were the offspring of John and Jane Castree from Sedgeley who had sons called William, John, Edwin and Charles; the sons of Charles and Mary Castree from Orcop included James, George, William and Jeremiah, whilst a third couple, John and Eliza from Orcop, had sons David and Charles. Which of these are the ones in the photographs is not known.

Duffety is another surname that is repeated in the albums, though this time there are only two prisoners so named. Gilbert Duffety was first photographed in 1901 but returned again the following year, this time with a Dennis Duffety, who would seem to be his father. However, the 1891 census has Gilbert Duffety, aged eight, living with his family in Almondsbury, and the father is clearly named as Tenant Duffety, a licensed hawker. It is debatable whether Dennis and Tenant are one and the same man. Their crime, in 1902, was stealing 64lbs of hay for which they were both sentenced to six weeks in jail plus hard labour. At the time, Dennis was a fifty-year-old labourer, born in Bristol and professing to be a member of the Church of England, and Gilbert was a nineteen-year-old mop and skewer maker, born in Henbury near Bristol and of the same church.

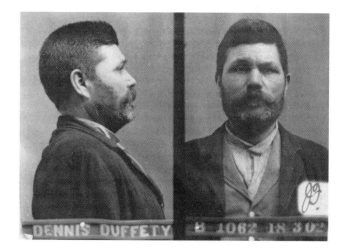

Dennis Duffety, 18 March 1902.

Gilbert Duffety, 10 July 1901 and 18 March 1902.

There seems to be a family likeness between the three photographs of Griffiths men, for Edward, James and Nehemiah, taken in the gaol between 1885 and 1893 but, as the name is relatively common and no further details are available on the men, it is impossible to say if they are definitely related. There was also a minor called Raymond Griffiths.

The final surname that is repeated and where the photographs seem to show a family resemblance is that of Chandler, a well-known Gloucestershire name. There are four photographs of Chandler men, two each for George and James Chandler (only one shown here) and there was one photograph of an Elizabeth Chandler (see Women Prisoner's section). Additionally, there was a record in 1870 but no photograph for a Thomas Chandler, a thirty-six-year-old married collier, who was sentenced to fourteen days with hard labour for stealing cider. It is possible that Elizabeth is the wife of one of the men rather than a sister, and there is indeed a married couple with forenames George and Elizabeth in the Stroud area in 1901, but there is no proof that it is this particular couple or that there is any link whatsoever between the three people.

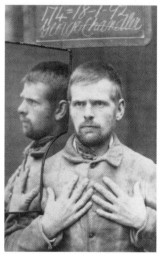 

Clockwise from left
James Chandler, 26 August 1889 and 31 December 1895.

George Chandler, 18 January 1892 and 13 April 1895.

Edward Griffiths, 20 February 1888 and 23 October 1890.

James Griffiths, 15 April 1893.

Nehemiah Griffiths, 11 April 1885.

eight

WORLDWIDE PRISONERS

Surprisingly, Gloucester Gaol has been the temporary home to a handful of petty criminals from places around the world rather than just from the county of Gloucestershire; they came from America, Australia, Canada, France, Germany, Italy, Malta, New Zealand, Norway, Poland and Switzerland.

Records remain for William E.F. Hall who originated from Australia, Charles Lang from Germany, Andrew Marini, born in Italy, Sevan Olson, born in Norway, and George Pyser, born in Poland, but they are in the section of the first album that does not include photographs.

William Hall was a child of ten years old and a labourer when he was recorded in Gloucester Gaol on 29 April 1870. He was charged with stealing a fowl and sentenced to twenty-one days with hard labour followed by five years at Reformatory. His intention, when his sentence was completed, was to return to Bourton on the Hill.

Born around 1834 in Germany, Charles Lang was remanded in Gloucester Gaol in 1869. A single man, Charles worked as a hawker and was found guilty of stealing pictures along with another man, George Pyser, for which offence they were sentenced to six months with hard labour. When he was released, Charles' intention was to quit the county and head for London. George Pyser, a twenty-nine-year-old married cap-maker born in Poland, was heading for Liverpool.

Andrew Marini was a twenty-four-year-old unmarried seaman from Italy who was charged with malicious wounding and sentenced to fourteen days with hard labour. He had no plans for what he would do on his release.

Sevan (Sven?) Olsen was a twenty-three-year-old seaman from Norway photographed in Gloucester Gaol on 30 April 1870. His crime was stealing a bag, for which he was sentenced to five days of hard labour. He was uncertain as to where he would go on his release.

There are two photographs of men who, from their names, would appear to be from foreign parts, but for whom no information to that effect is available. They were Bernhard Piepho and Louis Delavaux or Delavous.

Above, from left Josiah Cunningham came to England from America where he was born around 1866. As he gives no more accurate details of his birthplace, it is impossible to find a more precise location for his origin or his family background. His trade was that of a corn porter so it is suspected that he came to the port of Gloucester where that commodity was handled. Josiah had his photograph taken on 23 June 1902 after being found guilty of stealing three ropes, 124lbs of iron bolts and 71lbs of nails for which he received the sentence of three calendar months in gaol with hard labour. He said he was a member of the Church of England

Henry William Southey was only eighteen when he was imprisoned in Gloucester Gaol in 1903. Born in Australia, Henry was a seaman and presumably arrived at Gloucester Docks. His crime, for which he was sentenced to three calendar months with hard labour, was obtaining goods by false pretences. Occasionally, Henry used the aliases of Harry Green and Harry Carter.

Three men who claimed to be born in Canada made their way to Gloucester: Thomas Grant in 1870, Fonier King in 1902–03 and Alfred Bell Croxson in 1904–05. Thomas Grant looks rather bemused to find himself in this situation! He was a single man working as a labourer. He was sentenced to six weeks with hard labour for stealing boots. His intention when he was released was to go to North Cerney, which presumably was where he was working when he committed his offence.

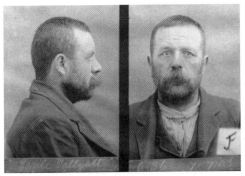

Above, left and right Emile Vallyatt, a Roman Catholic, said that he was born in Paris in France when he was committed to Gloucester Gaol in 1903. Emile was a baker aged forty-five. His crime was stealing two motor car lamps and he was sentenced to one calendar month with hard labour. His partner in crime at the time of this offence was one Vincent Ferrari, an Italian-born sailor, who was given the same sentence. Vincent was younger than Emile, being thirty-two years old, but was also a Roman Catholic. The photographs were taken on 7 July 1903.

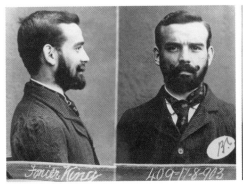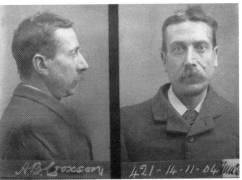

Above, from left Fonier King was committed twice to Gloucester Gaol, once in 1902 and again the following year. His first crime was obtaining wearing apparel by false pretences for which he was sentenced to four calendar months with hard labour. There are no details found for his second crime. Born around 1874 in Canada, Fonier was one of the few professional men held in the prison; he was a civil engineer.

Alfred Bell Croxson also appeared twice in the photograph albums. He claimed to have been born in Toronto, Canada, around 1864, but was he telling the truth? There is, on the 1871 census, an Alfred B. Croxson aged seven years old living with his widowed mother, West Croxson, and two siblings in Leigh, Essex. On that record, he was recorded as being born in Portsmouth. There is also an entry in the General Register Office indexes to births for an Alfred Bell Croxson in the first quarter of 1864 in the Portsea district. Perhaps he was actually telling the truth – he could have been born in Canada just before his mother returned to her roots when she registered him in the United Kingdom. Alfred was a clerk who was sentenced to six weeks with hard labour for larceny 'after a PCF', believed to be some sort of caution. Occasionally Alfred used the alias of Walter Richards. There is no available information on his second offence.

Above, from left Arthur Kerridge, born in Germany, was twenty-four years old when he was photographed in Gloucester Gaol on 3 November 1903. Arthur worked as a valet and was charged with committing burglary and stealing one silver ingot and a wedding ring. For this comparatively serious crime, Arthur was sentenced to twelve calendar months with hard labour.

Isaac Hudd was another prisoner who seems to have been unsure about his origins. He was a shoemaker who purported to have been born in Malta around 1875; however, on the 1891 census, there is an Isaac Hudd, also a shoemaker, this time aged nineteen, so born around 1872, held in Lawford's Gate House of Correction, who must surely be the same man. This Isaac Hudd said he was born in St George's parish on the outskirts of Bristol. Isaac was photographed in Gloucester Gaol on 14 August 1899. His crime was stealing nine fowls, breaking into a warehouse and stealing seven pair of boot uppers, etc. He was found guilty of the offence and sentenced to twelve months with hard labour.

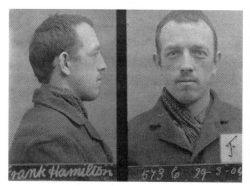

Above, from left Frank Richard Hamilton stated that he was born in New Zealand when his details were taken on arrival at the prison. Twenty-six years old in 1904, Frank was a mental nurse who was also a member of the Church of England. His crime was stealing money, for which he was sentenced to six calendar months with hard labour and three years police supervision. He had no specific destination on completion of his sentence.

Edward Schmid was another of the professional men held in the gaol; he was a dentist born in Switzerland around 1870. His offence was obtaining board and lodgings by false pretences and when found guilty, he was sentenced to one month of hard labour. His photograph was taken on 29 March 1902.

Bernhard Piepho was photographed in
soldier's uniform on 14 October 1889.

Louis Delavaux was photographed on
27 March 1886.

nine

THE IRISH, THE SCOTS
AND THE WELSH

Many prisoners came from less distant shores than the continents of America, Australia or Europe but were, nonetheless, from places quite far from Gloucester. Beginning in Ireland, we find three prisoners entered in the 1870 album who do not have photographs.

Mary May, a married woman born in Ireland around 1825, was charged twice in April and May 1870 for stealing a coat and then for stealing a dress. She was first sentenced to six weeks gaol with hard labour and then for another twenty-one days of the same. She planned to go to Cheltenham on her release.

Another Irish woman in gaol at the same time was Margaret Yeates. A married woman aged forty-two, Margaret's crime was stealing meat. She was given a sentence of ten days with hard labour and afterwards release to go to Campden.

Cornelius O'Leary was a twenty-nine-year-old married labourer found guilty of stealing coal in 1870. He was sentenced to six weeks in gaol with hard labour. His destination on release was Lydney.

Jeremiah Madden gave Ireland as his birthplace when he was photographed in 1870. He was a single, fifty-year-old labourer sentenced to two months with hard labour for stealing iron. On his release, he planned to go to Coleford.

Opposite below, from left James Green claimed Belfast as his birthplace when he was jailed in 1904. He was a thirty-three-year-old French polisher and a member of the Church of England. His crime was begging and he was found guilty and sentenced to ten days with hard labour.

Thomas Murphy was a Roman Catholic who came from Cork in the south of Ireland where he was born around 1881. He was twenty years old in 1901 when he was found guilty of stealing a coat and sentenced to one calendar month in gaol with hard labour.

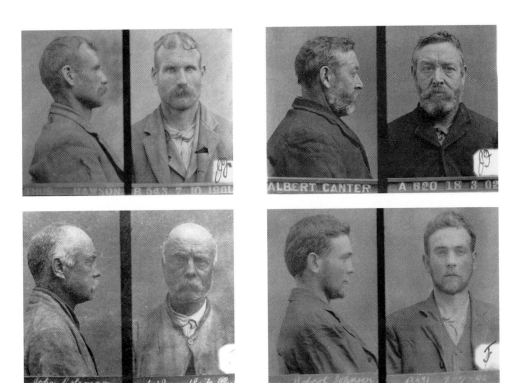

Top row, from left Thomas Dawson, alias Thomas Dalton, was thirty-six years old when photographed in 1901. An Irish labourer and a Roman Catholic, Thomas' crime was to be caught in an outhouse with, supposedly, intent to steal chickens. His sentence was seven days of hard labour.

Albert Canter was also known as Michael Feiney, John Matthews and Thomas Arnett so was obviously a very seasoned offender in 1902 at the age of twenty-seven. A labourer and a Roman Catholic, he was given a six-month sentence for stealing two dozen glass tumblers.

Second row John Coleman was one of the older prisoners photographed, aged sixty-two, on 18 July 1902. He was caught stealing a lady's jacket and sentenced to twenty-one days of hard labour. John stated that he was a member of the Church of England.

Robert Johnson also claimed to be a member of the Church of England. He was a twenty-seven-year-old window cleaner. Guilty of stealing an overcoat, a handkerchief, a piece of mutton and a purse in 1902, Robert was given a sentence of twenty-one days with hard labour.

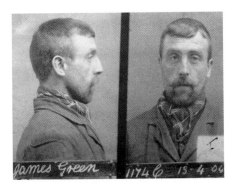

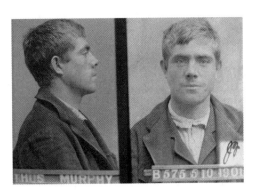

Originating in Scotland were Clara Ewbank (see the section on Women Prisoners), John Thompson, Alexander Mackay, George Tudhope, Henry Macdonald and Henry Wingrove.

John Thompson was recorded but not photographed in the first album in 1870 as being a thirty-six-year-old engine driver from Glasgow. His crime was stealing tools and he was given a sentence of nine months with hard labour. On his release, he planned to go to Birmingham. There was a note with his record stating that he had been in the Scottish Greys, otherwise known as the Royal Scots Greys or the 2nd Dragoons.

Above, from left George Tudhope was thirty years old in 1904 and a member of the Church of England, but his religion did not prevent him from committing the sin of attempting suicide, for which he was jailed for seven days with hard labour. George was a married watchman, born in Millerhill on the outskirts of Edinburgh, who gave no indication of his destination on release from Gloucester Gaol.

Also in gaol in 1904 was Henry McDonald. He was a stoker from Glasgow, aged twenty-four, who occasionally used the alias of Ernest Holton. Henry's crime was the stealing of a china tea service and some tools. He was sentenced to three months with hard labour.

Henry Wingrove was a single man, born in Leith around 1822. In 1870, he found himself being photographed in Gloucester Gaol for the crime of stealing a bottle of porter. A cabinet maker by trade, Henry received a sentence of ten days with hard labour. On his release, Henry was heading for Thornbury.

A bit closer to home were the prisoners who came from Wales. There were three recorded in gaol in 1870 for whom no pictures survive.

William Clayton was a single man, aged forty, who was given seven days with hard labour for stealing timber. He planned to go to the western part of the Forest of Dean on his release.

James Jarvis was born in North Wales around 1819. A married man and a nailer by trade, James was given seven days hard labour for stealing rabbits. He planned to go to Cirencester on his release.

John Millington specified Bangor in North Wales as his birthplace around 1840. John was given six weeks hard labour for stealing forks. A chemist by profession, John was uncertain where he would go on his release and the record stated that he would be a tramp.

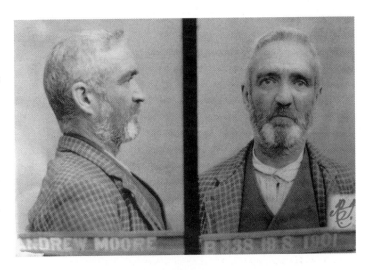

Andrew Moore was fifty-four years old when he was photographed in Gloucester Gaol in August 1901. He was a pedlar from Wrexham in North Wales and claimed to be a member of the Church of England. His crime was somewhat more serious than most of the criminals housed with him; he was given a sentence of twelve months with hard labour for 'attempting carnal knowledge of a girl'.

Arthur Thomas Watkins was a member of the Wesleyan faith and was thirty-two years old when recorded in 1903. A collier from Monmouthshire, Arthur was sentenced to ten calendar months with hard labour followed by three years of police supervision for stealing a bicycle.

Four people claimed their birth was in Cardiff: Alice Foley and Elizabeth Milton (see section on Women Prisoners), George Jameson and John Ward.

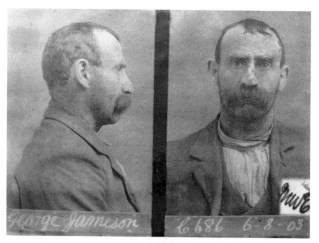

George Jameson's crime was stealing a silver watch for which he was sentenced to twelve calendar months with hard labour. George was a thirty-five-year-old dealer, born in Cardiff around 1868 and a member of the Church of England. It appears that, at some stage, his photograph was stepped on as it is rather muddy in places.

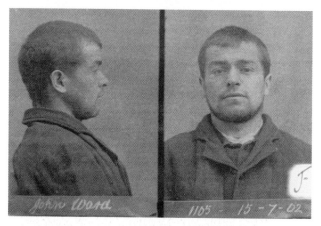

John Ward, a labourer and a member of the Church of England, was born around 1878 in Cardiff, according to his gaol record. Photographed twice, on 25 February 1902 and, five months later, on 15 July 1902, John was charged with stealing two overcoats. He was sentenced to four calendar months with hard labour.

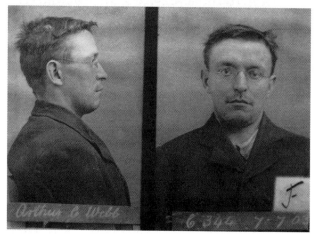

Arthur Clifford Webb came from Abergavenny. He was thirty years old in 1903 when he was charged with money laundering or 'fraudulent conversion of money received on account of other persons' and sentenced to one month in gaol with hard labour. Arthur was a member of the Church of England and a compositor by trade.

ten

BRISTOL PRISONERS

Getting closer to home, there were twenty prisoners who gave Bristol as their birth place but not all of them have images to go with their records. The first of these was Henry Winniatt, who was the first man to be photographed in the gaol in April 1870. Others include:

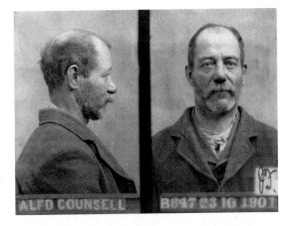

Alfred Counsell, a forty-eight-year-old labourer who, in 1901, was given a sentence of one calendar month in gaol with hard labour for stealing a pair of boots.

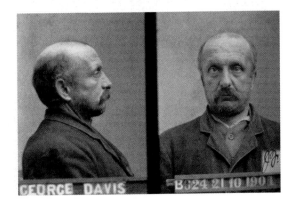

A forty-five year-old-hawker, George Davis was also given a one month sentence in 1901, this time for stealing seven pairs of socks.

Francis Garland was a forty-five-year-old plasterer when he received his sentence in 1901 of one month with hard labour for maliciously damaging a house.

John Marlow was given a month's gaol with hard labour in 1901 for stealing clock weights. He was a forty-three-year-old labourer who claimed to be a member of the Church of England.

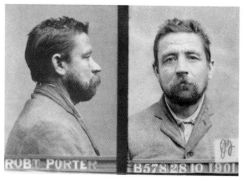

Robert Porter was John Marlow's partner-in-crime. Another labourer, he was two years younger than Marlow.

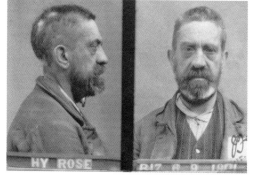

Henry Rose, aged fifty and a labourer, committed the crime of robbery with violence in 1901 and was given a three-month sentence with hard labour.

Alfred Henry Tucker was thirty-six years old when he set fire to a stable and barn. A porter by occupation, his case was sent to the Assizes in November 1902.

Henry Purnell, a collier, was found guilty of stealing three ropes, 124lbs of iron bolts and 71lb of nails for which crime he was given six calendar months in gaol with hard labour. He was thirty-two years old in 1902 when he was photographed. His partner in crime was the American, Josiah Cunningham.

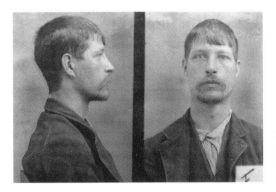

Ernest White came from Kingswood, Bristol. He was a bootmaker, aged twenty-eight, sentenced in 1903 to nine months with hard labour for stealing leather.

George Hendy also claimed Kingswood near Bristol as his place of birth. He was born there around 1864 and became a shoemaker by trade. George broke into a warehouse and stole boots and leather uppers for which crime he was sentenced in 1903, to six weeks with hard labour.

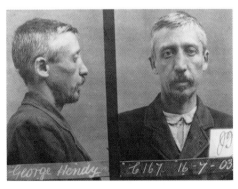

eleven

GLOUCESTERSHIRE PRISONERS

Of the 500 or so prisoners who recorded their place of birth in the registers, almost exactly half originated in Gloucestershire itself, not including those who listed Bristol as their birth place. The place from which most of the inmates came was Cheltenham (26), followed by Gloucester (12) and then Stroud (5).

Roger O'More was thirty-four years old when he was photographed in Gloucester Gaol on 14 August 1899. He claimed to have been born in Dursley and to be a member of the Church of England. Described as 5ft 6in tall, Roger had brown hair and was, according to his record, an 'old Reformatory boy' and 'convict'. He was a coach painter by trade and, at the Assizes, was given a fifteen-month sentence with hard labour for burglary. According to his entry in the register of previous convictions, Roger had a criminal record going back twenty-one years, to when he was only thirteen years old, and seems to have spent much of his life behind bars. Occasionally, he used the aliases of Henry Higgins and George Harris. His list of crimes includes:

Year	Location	Crime	Sentence
1879	Dursley	Stealing cakes	10 days & 3 yrs Reformatory
1882	Gloucester	Stealing a coat	2 months
1884	Gloucester	False pretences	3 months
1885	Gloucester	Stealing workbox & £36	12 months
1885	Gloucester	Stealing purse	6 months
1886	Gloucester	Obtaining position with forged character	2 months
1888	Dursley	Exposing his person	14 days
1890	Gloucester	Demanding money with	5 yrs penal servitude
1896	Dursley	Exposing his person (6 times)	2 months each (consecutive)
1897	Bristol	Uttering counterfeit coin	6 months
1898	Gloucester	Burglary	15 months
1900	Plymouth	Stealing a gold ring, chain	6 months
1900	Bridgwater	Larceny	3 yrs penal servitude
1903	Cheltenham	Failing to report to police	3 months

Roger O'More, 14 August 1899.

Year	Location	Crime	Sentence
1904	Gloucester	Incorrigible rogue	12 months & 12 strokes of birch
1906	Gloucester	Exposing his person	12 months
1907	Gloucester	Exposing his person	12 months & 12 strokes of birch

Roger's crimes continued and varied from the petty to the serious, when he was found guilty of shooting with intent to do grievous bodily harm. At this point he was sent to Gloucester County Asylum to check his sanity but was discharged after a month and returned to the gaol.

David O'Hagan was another petty criminal to appear in the Previous Convictions register. His criminal record began in 1883 when he was twenty-five years old and lasted for more than thirty years. His travels took him several times from Bristol to Cheltenham, Gloucester, Worcester, Usk, and Glamorgan. His crimes ranged from embezzlement, stealing food, clothing and money, malicious damage to drunkenness, begging and sleeping rough, and the sentences he received stretched from seven days with hard labour to three years of penal servitude. David did not seem to be sure of his origins as both Cheltenham and Cardiff are listed as possible places of birth and he was equally unsure of his religion, giving both Roman Catholic and Church of England!

David O'Hagan, 30 April 1901.

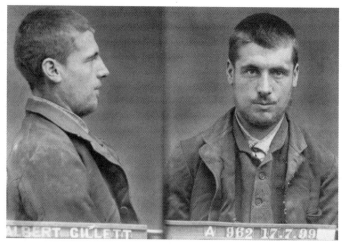

Above, from left John Essex was twenty-one and a labourer when he was held in Gloucester Gaol in 1870. His crime was a serious one of robbery with violence, for which he was given eighteen months in gaol with hard labour. He was born in Rodborough about 1847, the fourth child of John and Elizabeth Essex who lived in Houndscroft.

Albert Gillett came from Down Ampney but found himself in jail in 1902 for having committed a burglary. He was sentenced to twelve months with hard labour. This was at least his third offence as he was also photographed there in 1899 and 1900.

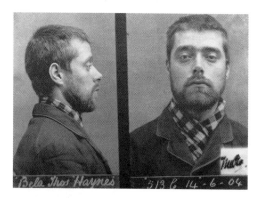

Above, from left Another man to be photographed more than once was one with the unusual name of Bela Thomas Haynes. He appeared in 1903 and 1904, charged both times with housebreaking. In the earlier charge, he was also accused of stealing a pair of boots. Aged twenty-four, Bela was a brickmaker born in the village of Bourton-on-the-Water. His sentences for the two crimes were six and nine months in prison with hard labour.

James Gwilliam was thirty years old when he was jailed in 1903. His unusual crime was 'forging a request for the delivery of goods' for which he was sentenced to six months in gaol with hard labour. James was a collier who gave his birth place as Beckford.

Opposite Twenty-six-year-old John Morefield was born in Sandhurst, Gloucestershire, around 1844, the son of Thomas and Eliza Morefield. John was given a twenty-day sentence for stealing potatoes. A married man, John was heading for Hull when he was released.

Above, from left George Cox was thirty-two years old in 1870 when his photograph was taken in gaol. Born in Cam, George was a plasterer who was found guilty of the arson of a shed and was sentenced to eighteen months with hard labour.

A basket maker from Cirencester, Henry Matthew Paish was sentenced to twelve months with hard labour for housebreaking and stealing. Unmarried and twenty-one years of age when photographed in 1870, Henry planned to head for Tetbury when he was released. Arrested at Chedworth, Henry was tried at Gloucester. He was 5ft 2in tall with light brown hair and grey eyes, which were said to be weak. He had a previous conviction for stealing potatoes. Earlier in the same year, a twenty-year-old labourer called Charles Paish, also from Cirencester, was held in the gaol for stealing bags. His sentence was one month in gaol. There is no photograph of Charles.

James Webley hailed from Dymock and was convicted at Newent Petty Sessions for stealing a scythe, an offence for which he was given a sentence of seven days with hard labour. Aged twenty-two, and born about 1848, James planned to return to Dymock where he was a labourer. He was 5ft 6in tall with brown hair and grey eyes and scars on his right knee and foot.

Right Arthur Jones was a miner from Littledean. Aged twenty-four in 1870, he was sentenced to six months with hard labour followed by three years under police supervision for stealing a duck and some fowl. A member of the Church of England, Arthur intended to return to the Forest of Dean when he was released from gaol.

Above, from left John Organ was a married man born in Badgeworth and aged twenty-six years when his photograph was taken in Gloucester Gaol in June 1870. He was 5ft 4in tall with dark brown hair and brown eyes. He had a mole on his left shoulder and a scar on his right hand. He was tried at Cheltenham Petty Sessions for stealing nails and was given a sentence of fourteen days with hard labour. He had no previous convictions.

Thomas Smith was born in Minchinhampton around 1844. He was 5ft 6in tall with dark hair and hazel eyes. He was distinguished by a long cut on his forehead, an anchor on his right hand and a ring on his second right finger. Thomas was arrested in his home town and tried at Gloucester Trinity Sessions where he was found guilty of horse stealing and sentenced to twelve months in gaol with hard labour. He was a married labourer and planned to go to Stroud on his release. Thomas had a previous conviction for wilful damage in 1867 for which he served two months.

Samuel Jordan, born in Tewkesbury, was a twenty-seven-year-old single labourer when he was tried at Gloucester Assizes on 9 August 1869 for 'feloniously receiving'. He was given a nine-month sentence with hard labour. Samuel was just 5ft tall, had brown hair, grey eyes a sallow complexion and a scar on his upper lip. Samuel had eight previous convictions and was described on his record as 'an associate of thieves and poachers'. Samuel, a member of the Church of England, intended to stay in Gloucester on his release from gaol.

Left Robert Hulls stated that he was forty-seven years old and born in Gloucester when he was brought before the Gloucester Trinity Sessions on 1 July 1869 for the crime of 'feloniously receiving stolen goods'. Robert, a single labourer, was given a sentence of twelve months with hard labour. The severity of the sentence was due to his eight previous convictions, one for using threats and seven for poaching. The record states that he was a 'very bad character'. Described as 5ft 7in tall with grey hair, grey eyes and a fresh complexion, Robert had a cut on the bridge of his nose and cupping scars on the back of his neck.

Above, left Richard Hooper was a single labourer, aged forty-six, when he was arrested and sent before the Gloucester Quarter Sessions for stealing brass. He was given a sentence of three months with hard labour. A single man born in Cirencester around 1824, Richard was 5ft 4in tall, had sandy coloured hair, blue eyes and a light complexion. He was also in the unfortunate position of having lost all his teeth.

Opposite, from far left Francis Deal was born in Cheltenham about 1836. He was married and a sawyer by trade. He was sentenced at Cheltenham Petty Sessions on 2 April 1870 for stealing saws and was given six weeks in gaol with hard labour. He was 5ft 5in tall with brown hair, brown eyes, a dark complexion and a scar on his right eyebrow. Francis planned to return to his family in Cheltenham on his release.

George Holder had 'hitherto borne a good character' when he was brought before Stroud Petty Sessions in March 1870, charged with stealing a gun. Born in Chalford around 1833, George was described as 5ft 10in tall with brown hair, grey eyes and a pale complexion. He also suffered a contracted left elbow. George was a single man at that time and a waterman by trade. He intended to return to his home village when he was released after serving two months with hard labour.

Thomas Pates was a forty-four-year-old married gardener when, in 1870, he found himself in front of the magistrates at Cheltenham Petty Sessions, charged with stealing a scythe and a billhook from his master. Thomas, described as being pockmarked, 5ft 5in tall with dark brown hair, brown eyes and with a fresh complexion, was given a sentence of one month with hard labour. No previous convictions were recorded.

Aged forty-four years, James Reeves was described as being 5ft 2in tall with brown hair, blue eyes and a fresh complexion. He also suffered a contracted fourth finger on his right hand. When he was brought before the magistrates at Campden Petty Sessions on 6 April 1870, he was charged with stealing barley. Found guilty, James, a married labourer from Blockley, was given a sentence of two months in gaol with hard labour, despite having no previous convictions. His intention on leaving the gaol on 4 June 1870 was to return to his home village.

Above, from left Appearing at Newnham Petty Sessions on 16 May 1870, William Cooper was found guilty of stealing hay and was given one month of hard labour in Gloucester Gaol. Aged forty-eight and born in Littledean, William had, ten years previously, served nine months in Gloucester Gaol for sheep stealing. William was a married man and a collier; he was described as 5ft 6in tall with dark brown hair, hazel eyes and a fresh complexion. On his release, William planned to return to the Forest of Dean.

Another forty-eight-year-old in the gaol in 1870 was John Cooper, seemingly no relation to the previous convict. John was born in Thornbury and was a single labourer. His crime was stealing a hay knife and for that he was sentenced at Thornbury Petty Sessions to one month in gaol with hard labour. John was described as 5ft 4in tall with brown hair, brown eyes and a ruddy complexion. He suffered an enlargement of the left shoulder. John had no fixed residence at the time and was uncertain where he would go on his release. He was 'not known in this county being a tramp'.

Mark Wheeler also stated that he was born in Thornbury. He was fifty-six years old in 1870 when he was jailed at Gloucester Quarter Sessions for six months with hard labour for stealing timber. He was described as being 5ft 9in tall with grey hair and eyes and a fresh complexion with scars on his right wrist and left shin. Mark had three previous convictions by jury, one in 1843 for night poaching, for which he spent a year in gaol, followed in 1844 by a month in gaol for stealing an axe. But in 1852 he was given the much more severe sentence of seven years transportation for the very minor crime of stealing potatoes.

Another twenty-one-year-old was George Smith from the city of Gloucester itself. George was also a labourer. His crime was shop-breaking and stealing therein 'fifty-six metal 1lb checks'. He was sentenced to six months in gaol with hard labour and photographed there on 25 September 1903. George professed to be a member of the Church of England.

Henry Wilkes was a soldier in 1902 when he was found guilty of stealing money and jewellery. Aged twenty-two and born in Gloucester, Henry was given a sentence of six calendar months with hard labour.

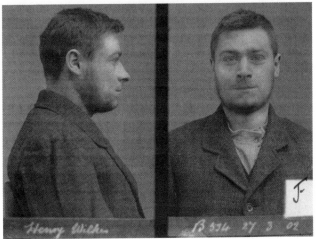

Opposite below, from far left John James was 5ft 9in in height with brown hair, hazel eyes and a fresh complexion. He had obviously had a few injuries in his life as he had a long scar down his right leg, a scar on his left shoulder and a blue scar on his right arm. John was twenty-two years old when he appeared before Gloucester Assizes on 30 March 1870 on a charge of assault. A single man, born in Lydney, John was given a sentence of three months with hard labour. This was John's second offence of assault and he was recorded as being 'a notorious poacher'. On his release, John intended to return to the Forest of Dean.

Nathaniel Clements was thirty-three years old when, at Stroud Petty Sessions in 1870, he was given one month in gaol with hard labour for stealing meat. Nathaniel professed not to know his birth place but the 1851 census suggests it was Rodborough, where he was arrested. He was described as having brown hair, grey eyes and a fresh complexion and being 5ft 7in tall. He had a brown mark on the back of his neck and a scar on his left cheek. Nathaniel was a stonemason by trade and had no previous convictions.

George Soule, a thirty-one-year-old married shoemaker, born in Painswick, was tried at the Whitminster Petty Sessions on 7 April 1870 when he was found guilty of stealing coals. George had brown hair and eyes, a fresh complexion and cupping scars on his shoulder; he was 5ft 3in tall. After serving his sentence of one month with hard labour, George intended to go to live in Stonehouse.

Above, from left George Hooper came from Moreton-in-Marsh where he was born around 1880. A labourer, George committed the crime of sheep stealing and was sentenced to eight calendar months with hard labour followed by three years under police supervision.

Born in Cheltenham around 1879, George Kear was a painter who committed forgery. For that he was sentenced to four months with hard labour in 1902.

Adolphus Daniel Young was photographed twice, once in 1900 and again in 1902. His crime in the latter instance was indecent assault and obstructing the police. Aged twenty-two and a labourer from Stroud, Adolphus was sentenced to eight calendar months with hard labour.

Above, from left A prisoner with a most unusual name was Ivo Vane Porter. Born in 1880 in Aldsworth to George and Elizabeth Porter, Ivo found a job as a postman but ended up in Gloucester Gaol in 1904, having been found guilty of 'larceny whilst employed under the Post Office'. He was sentenced to four months in gaol with hard labour.

Edward George Andrews was twenty-five years old when he had his photograph taken in Gloucester Gaol on 29 March 1904. He had been transferred from Ipswich Prison. His crime was stealing timber and tools. A fishmonger born in Cheltenham, and claiming to be a member of the Church of England, Edward was given a sentence of six calendar months with hard labour.

Frederick William Nicholls was photographed twice, first time in 1900 then later in 1902. Coming from Brockworth on the outskirts of Gloucester, Frederick was found guilty of stealing a waterproof coat. Born around 1877, Frederick was a baker and received a sentence of eight months with hard labour for his crime.

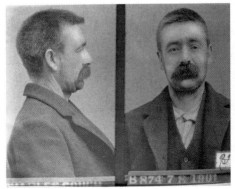
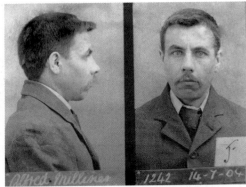
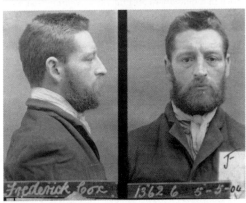

Clockwise from above Born in Ashleworth around 1872, Charles Gough was a labourer and twenty-nine years of age when he was arrested in 1901. His crime was 'attempting to carnally know an imbecile woman' and for this he was sentenced to two months with hard labour.

Alfred Ernest Milliner was born in Tockington near Olveston around 1874. A member of the Church of England, Alfred was convicted of a felony – larceny in a dwelling house in 1904. A bricklayer, Alfred was sentenced to six months with hard labour.

Frederick Charles Cox gave his religion as Dissenter but didn't specify which faith he belonged to. He was found guilty of stealing lead in 1904 and sentenced to six weeks with hard labour. Born in Cheltenham around 1874, Frederick was a labourer.

Opposite below, from far left Philip Hatton was a mason's labourer from Newnham. He was photographed in 1901 when he was sentenced to two months with hard labour for indecent assault. He was twenty-seven years old at the time. With dark brown hair and at 5ft 6in tall, Philip was committed at Littledean and sent to the Assizes for trial. His record states that he was a member of the Church of England, had no previous convictions and had an imperfect education.

William Iles was a twenty-two-year-old soldier born in Cheltenham. William was charged with stealing two plates, two knives, etc. He was sentenced to three calendar months with hard labour in 1902 for his crime. William was a member of the Church of England.

James Thomas Cox came from Kemble. He was a labourer, sentenced to six months with hard labour for having maliciously thrown stones at a railway carriage. He was twenty-eight when his photograph was taken in December 1902.

Above, from left George Nash was thirty years old in 1902 when he was found guilty of indecent assault and given a sentence of three calendar months with hard labour. A labourer, George claimed to have been born in Cheltenham.

William Phillips originated in Newent around 1871 and was working as a grocer's assistant in 1901 when he was charged with embezzling £1. He was sentenced to six weeks with hard labour.

Above, from left Aged thirty-three when arrested in 1903 for stealing clothes, Frederick Fry was a labourer from Chalfield. His sentence was a month in Gloucester Gaol with hard labour.

Robert Andrews was a fitter born in Gloucester around 1867. In 1901, he was charged with stealing a bag and £26 from the Midland Railway Co. He was given a sentence of six weeks with hard labour.

Jacob Newman came from Mangotsfield where he was born around 1866. He was a thirty-six-year-old labourer when he was given a three-month sentence with hard labour for stealing one ring, a purse and 7s 6d.

Above, left and right James Osborne was a thirty-six-year-old shoemaker from Kingswood, though whether that was the Kingswood near Bristol or the one near Wotton-under-Edge is not known. His crime in 1903 was stealing a hammer and a brush for which he was given a two-month sentence with hard labour. The following year he was further charged with stealing lead. This time he was given three months. His partner in the latter crime was William Pool who was another shoemaker from Kingswood, aged thirty-seven. For some reason, maybe he was a first offender, but William only received a two-month sentence with hard labour for this crime.

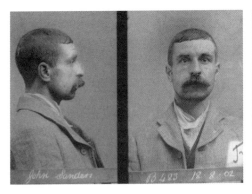

Above, from left John Sanders was a labourer born around 1865 in Cheltenham. He was found guilty of stealing a hair-clipping machine and sentenced to fourteen days in gaol or a fine of £1 14s.

Frederick Henry Stephens was born in Gloucester around 1864. He was a labourer charged with obtaining a suit of clothes by false pretences, and sentenced to one calendar month with hard labour.

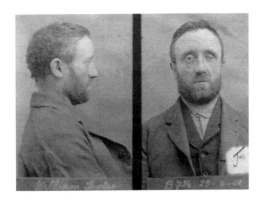

William Taylor was born in Prestbury around 1864 and was a hawker. In 1902 when he was thirty-eight years old, William was charged with stealing a horse, a dog and a rug. For his crime, he was sentenced to four calendar months with hard labour.

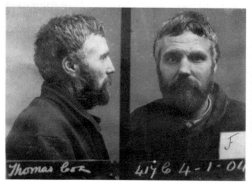

Above, from left Thomas Cox actually had his photograph taken three times, in 1900, 1902 and 1904, so was obviously a repeat offender. His crime in 1900 is not recorded but in the other two instances, he was charged with 'exposing his person' and being 'an incorrigible rogue', two terms which seem to be synonymous. In 1902 Thomas was sentenced to twelve months hard labour and, two years later, three months in gaol. He was born in Tetbury around 1861 and was a labourer.

William Humphries came from Kingstanley. He was a blacksmith by trade and, in October 1902, he was photographed in Gloucester Gaol where he had been sent for a month with hard labour for stealing three chickens. He was forty-three at the time.

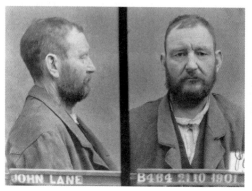

Above, from left John Lane was a labourer born in Ashleworth around 1856. In 1901, he was jailed for a month with hard labour, also for stealing three chickens.

Henry Bigwood's record stated that he was jailed for five months with hard labour followed by two years under police supervision. His crime was 'stealing 4s 6d in money after PCF'. The latter is thought to be a police caution. Henry came from Warmley in the south of the county. He was a forty-six-year-old labourer when his details were recorded at the end of 1904. He was also photographed in 1900.

Opposite below, from left Arthur Joel, a labourer, came from Siddington near Cirencester where he was born around 1847. Arthur was given a six-month gaol sentence with hard labour for aiding and abetting someone else to steal 3s 9d.

George Frederick Skipp was fifty-six years old and born in Gloucester. He was an engineer by trade who was photographed in the gaol on 19 August 1904. George's crime was stealing a knife, spoon, bread and a jacket. For this, he was given a twelve-month sentence in gaol with hard labour.

Above, from left George Court was a blacksmith from Newnham. Aged forty-six, in 1902 he was sentenced to four weeks with hard labour for breaking into a blacksmith's shop and stealing therein a hammer, a file, etc.

James Michael Lugg was a dealer from Bisley. Born around 1855, James was forty-seven years old when his photograph was taken in Gloucester Gaol in March 1902. His crime was 'forging an endorsement on an order for £41', for which he was sentenced to two months with hard labour.

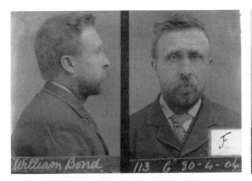

Above, from left William Bond was a clock maker by trade, born in Cinderford around 1856. He was photographed in Gloucester Gaol in 1904, having been found guilty of obtaining a watch by false pretences for which he served a sentence of twelve calendar months with hard labour.

It was 1 January 1900, the first day of the new century, when John Holloway was photographed in Gloucester Gaol. Born in Leckhampton around 1845, John was a gardener charged with larceny. His sentence was five months with hard labour. John was photographed again four years later; his crime this time is not recorded.

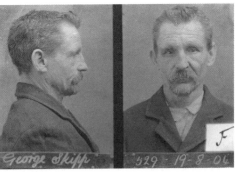

twelve

THE ENGLISH

Despite being told in school that our ancestors did not move around the country very much, a large proportion of the prisoners came from all corners of England. Indeed, from entries in the Previous Convictions registers, it is clear that many of them moved from place to place quite frequently. Quite a few appear to have come by water, either up the Bristol Channel to the port of Gloucester from Plymouth, Southampton, Southsea, London, Woolwich, Chatham and Liverpool, or down the River Severn from Stourport and Worcester.

A fifty-four-year-old widowed laundress from Plymouth, Jane Shellard, was sentenced to eighteen months with hard labour for stealing bedding – a very harsh sentence it would seem. Her destination, in 1870, was Cheltenham. Whether she was released into the community or not is unknown but, during her stay in gaol, the chaplain, H. Layton, recorded in his journal:

Visited Jane Shellard in padded cell. She has been raving mad this week arising from fits.

Perhaps she was sent to the asylum. She was not the only female prisoner to spend time in a padded cell as the minister recorded that he visited Sarah Britain and Emma Dyke there as well in April 1870.

At the same time in the gaol was fifty-two-year-old Mary Williams, a servant also hailing from Plymouth. Did they know each other? Mary's crime was cheating and she was given a much shorter sentence of one month with hard labour, and she was heading for St George's near Bristol as soon as she was free.

James Kingdom was a gardener who was born in Plymouth around 1845 and found in Gloucester Gaol twenty-five years later. He was accused of stealing a hoe and given a sentence of three months with hard labour. His destination on release was Horfield, near Bristol.

The two others who were born in the same place were John Henry William Livingstone and John Treeby.

There was no photograph taken of James Howard when he was in gaol in 1870. An unmarried seaman from Liverpool, born around 1842, he was obviously unable to earn enough to feed himself and was caught stealing bread, for which he was given a sentence of fourteen days in gaol with hard labour.

Above, from left John Livingstone was a sixteen-year-old tailor charged with stealing one sack, twenty-four glass bottles and 130lbs of rags, for which he was sentenced to three calendar months with hard labour. He stated that he was a Roman Catholic.

John Treeby, on the other hand, was a shoemaker aged thirty-four who was given a sentence of five calendar months with hard labour for breaking into a warehouse and stealing boots and leather uppers.

From further along the coast came Arthur West. He was a labourer and member of the Church of England, born in Devonport around 1866. Arthur's crime was to steal two overcoats and he was sentenced to three years of penal servitude. Whether he remained in the penitentiary section of Gloucester Gaol or was transferred to another, such as Pentonville Prison, is not known.

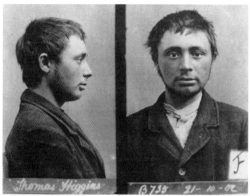

Above The other three prisoners who were born in Liverpool had no obvious connection with the sea. Thomas Higgins was a labourer aged twenty-one when he was imprisoned in October 1902, sentenced to fourteen days of hard labour for stealing a shirt. He was a Roman Catholic.

Right Also in the gaol in 1870 was George Parkinson, an unmarried cab driver, aged twenty-four. For stealing wearing apparel, he was sentenced to 'two months and four weeks hard labour'.

Above, from left Alfred Pope, a thirty-six-year-old plasterer, was sentenced to twenty-one days with hard labour for stealing a 2ft rule and a bottle of ink. A member of the Church of England, Alfred was obviously not content to stick to the name which he was given in Liverpool when he was born around 1866, as he used several aliases: Henry Atkins, Walter Jones, Thomas Jones and Henry Taylor.

One of the more unusual crimes committed by those featured in the albums was that of embezzlement. The final man from Liverpool was one John Spare Lewis, born in Liverpool around 1858. He married Annie Mary Young in the Petersfield district in 1881 and had a daughter Gertrude in 1883; eight years later, in 1891, the couple were living Chesterfield Road in the St James parish in Bristol when John was a bank clerk. By 1901, they had moved up in the world and were living in 'Highclere' in West Park and John had been promoted to bank manager. Very soon after, John fell from grace and was charged with embezzling £500, £130 and £100. He was sentenced to twelve months with hard labour. There is a suggestion in the records that John used the alias of Frederick Barber at some stage.

Above, from left From Southampton came Harriet Hancock Wyatt (see the Women Prisoners) and three labourers: William Barnes, Mark Nutburn and Henry Thompson. All claimed to be members of the Church of England. William Barnes was a forty-eight-year-old sentenced to twenty-one days with hard labour for stealing a ham.

Mark Nutburn was a twenty-eight-year-old labourer who stole a bag and seven fowls in 1902 and was sentenced to one month with hard labour. He stated that his religion was Church of England.

Over twenty prisoners claimed to have been born in London. Thirteen-year-old Charles Low, born about 1857 and unemployed, was sentenced to ten days imprisonment followed by a period at the Reformatory for stealing sweets. No photograph was taken of him, nor of Alfred John Walker, aged nineteen, who was a single labourer, found guilty of stealing a duck. He was sentenced to ten days with hard labour and released to go to Cheltenham. His details were entered into the Habitual Offenders register in August 1870.

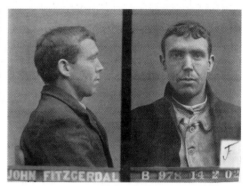

Above, from left Henry Thompson's crime was more violent than most. He was a twenty-four-year-old labourer, charged in 1902 with assaulting Sidney Timbrell and given a sentence of one calendar month with hard labour.

Next we have four prisoners who were born in the south-east of England. John Fitzgerald, a twenty-two year-old labourer from Chatham, occasionally used the alias Boxall. His crime was stealing a bag and seven fowls for which he was sentenced in early 1902 to one month in gaol with hard labour. John was a member of the Church of England.

Above, from left Three of the prisoners stated they were born in Woolwich, a tailor, a labourer and a seaman. William Fallows was a thirty-year-old tailor who, around 1901, made his way to Gloucester where he was gaoled for nine months with hard labour, for stealing jewellery. William was a Dissenter who sometimes used the alias of William Albert Pratt.

John Pelling was only nineteen years of age when he was arrested for stealing sheet lead, a crime for which he received a sentence of six weeks with hard labour in Gloucester Gaol. A labourer, John was a member of the Church of England.

Also born in Woolwich, around 1842, was Robert Herbert. Robert was a seaman and a member of the Church of England, charged in 1902 with the crime of attempted buggery for which he was given a six-month gaol sentence with hard labour.

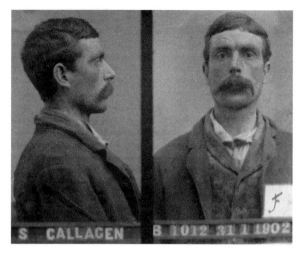

Aged thirty-two, Stephen Callaghan was a Roman Catholic, born in London according to his record. He was charged with stealing two pairs of boots and sentenced at the end of 1901 to fourteen days with hard labour.

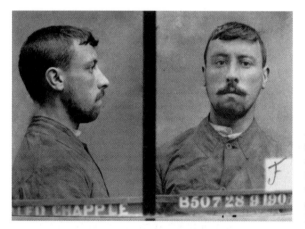

Alfred Chapple, a twenty-two-year-old seaman from London, stole two rugs and a shirt in 1901 and was sentenced to fourteen days in Gloucester Gaol with hard labour. He was recorded as being a member of the Church of England.

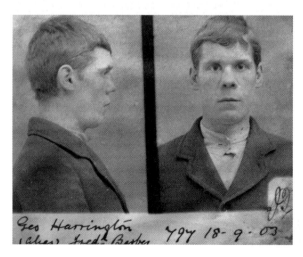

George Harrington was photographed twice, once in November 1902 and again ten months later in September 1903. He was twenty-one years old and a labourer. His crime was housebreaking and stealing from therein a piece of soap, a towel and a pack of cards. He was given twelve months with hard labour. George seems to have been a seasoned criminal as he was known by several aliases: Frank or Frederick Barber, George Brown and George Greenaway.

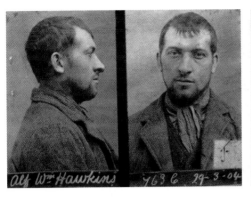
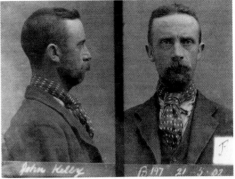

Above, from left Alfred William Hawkins was a woodchopper, aged twenty-three, from London. He was charged with housebreaking and given a sentence of six calendar months with hard labour. He was a member of the Church of England.

Stealing a ham was the crime committed by John Kelly, a thirty-year-old labourer who was born in London around 1872. He was sentenced to twenty-one days of hard labour.

Below, right George Kirk was an electrician. He was given a sentence of eight calendar months plus hard labour for the crime of shop-breaking and stealing shirts. Aged twenty-five in August 1902, he gave his birthplace as London.

Left William Knight was one of those photographed for the first album in 1870. He was just twenty years old, a single man and a labourer who was charged with stealing 9*d* from his master. He was apprehended at Woodside in the Forest of Dean and tried at Coleford on 17 May 1870, when he was sentenced to one month with hard labour. William was short for his age, at only 5ft tall. He had dark brown hair, hazel eyes, a fresh complexion and a scar on his forehead. His intention on being released was to go to Woolastone.

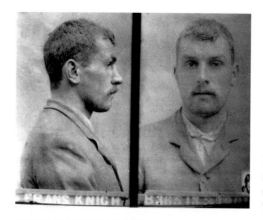

Francis Knight was arrested in 1901 and given a sentence of two months with hard labour for stealing 1s worth of bacon. He was a thirty-two-year-old labourer, born in London.

Thomas Littlby was a twenty-year-old from London who was accused of stealing 15s 10d and found guilty. He was imprisoned for three months with hard labour. Thomas was a car-man and recorded as being a member of the Church of England.

Charles Masters was a twenty-seven-year-old porter who said, according to the record in October 1904, that he was born in London. He was found guilty of stealing £1 10s and was given a sentence of one month in gaol.

Found guilty of obtaining board and lodging by false pretences, Charles Meridith was sentenced to four months in prison with hard labour. Charles was an electrical engineer, aged twenty-nine in 1902, who used the aliases of Charles Priest, George Fitzgerald and Thomas Schick.

Above, from left Leonard Montague was a porter who was born in London around 1878. He was arrested for stealing a china tea service and some tools, found guilty and sentenced to three months in prison with hard labour. He stated that he was a member of the Church of England.

George Morris, alias George Anthony Cox, broke into a counting house and stole lead piping. He was sentenced to six months with hard labour for his crime. Aged only eighteen at the time, in 1899, George was a labourer.

 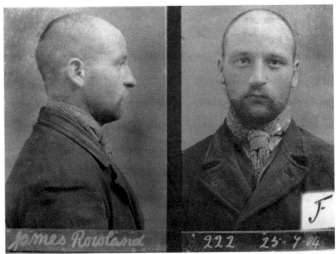

Above, from left Another eighteen-year-old from London was William Price. William was a single man and a clerk but he was arrested for burglary and sentenced to six months gaol with hard labour. On his release from Gloucester Gaol, he intended to go to Cheltenham.

James Rowland was thirty years old in 1904 when he was sentenced to two months with hard labour for breaking into stables and stealing a pair of clippers. James was a labourer and a member of the Church of England.

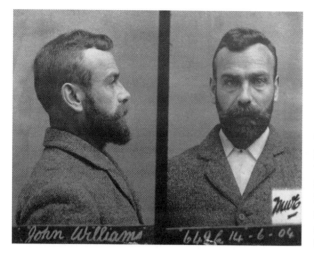

The last man who claimed to have been born in London was John Williams. In June 1904, John was twenty-eight years old and a seaman. His crime was one of false pretences and he was gaoled for nine calendar months plus hard labour when found guilty.

Edward Smith, born in London around 1878, was a labourer who stole two pairs of boots. A member of the Church of England, Edward was given a fourteen-day sentence with hard labour. His photograph was taken on the last day of January 1902.

Arthur White seems to have been a pickpocket as he was accused of 'stealing a silver watch from the person' and for this he was given a more severe punishment of five years penal servitude. It is possible that he served his sentence in the penitentiary section of Gloucester Gaol, but may have been transferred to another, such as Pentonville Prison, as many more serious offenders were. Arthur was twenty-six years old when he was photographed in January 1903.

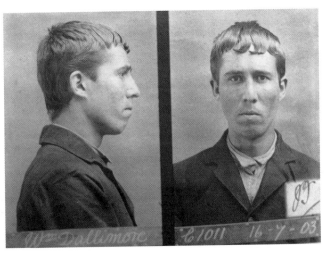

Above, from left In 1870, Frederick Brain was twenty-four years old and stated that he was born in Swindon. It doesn't actually specify if that was Swindon in Wiltshire or Swindon village near Cheltenham. A married man and a labourer, Frederick was charged with stealing a grindstone and was aptly sentenced to fourteen days with hard labour for his crime. His intention, on release, was to stay in Gloucester.

William Dallimore was born in Bath around 1882. He was a soldier when, in 1901, he was held in Gloucester Gaol serving a six-month sentence with hard labour for 'burglariously entering a dwelling house and stealing therein one clock'. William stated he was a member of the Church of England.

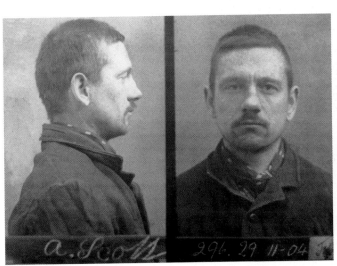

Above, from left Also from Bath was thirty-four-year-old Albert Scott. In 1904, Albert was found guilty of housebreaking and stealing therein, for which he was sentenced to six months in gaol with hard labour. A labourer, Albert said his religion was Church of England.

Henry Green said his place of birth was Berkshire but gave no specific location. Born around 1840, Henry was a gypsy hawker. In 1870, he was charged, with his wife Emma of whom there is no photograph, with receiving stolen property and sentenced to three months in gaol with hard labour.

In 1901, Joseph Fredericks, a groom from Birmingham, was to be found in Gloucester Gaol having been found guilty of stealing a set of harnesses. Aged twenty-three, Joseph was sentenced to twenty-one days with hard labour.

Thomas Martin was also from Birmingham. Born there around 1873, Thomas was a labourer who was found guilty of stealing a dog and sentenced to three months in gaol with hard labour. Occasionally, Thomas used the alias of Harrington.

Edward Morgan was an iron worker and a member of the Wesleyan faith. Aged twenty-seven, he was also born in Birmingham, around 1877. Edward was sentenced to twelve months with hard labour for obtaining food by false pretences.

From the south came William Ames, a forty-seven-year-old filmed in gaol on 25 November 1904. William was a sailor charged with obtaining charitable contributions under false pretences. His sentence was six months in gaol with hard labour, followed by two years under police supervision. William was a member of the Wesleyan religion, and born in Bournemouth..

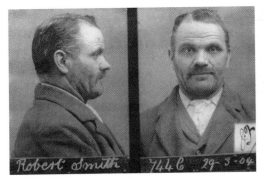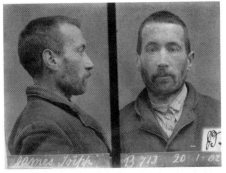

Above, from left Robert Smith was photographed twice, once in September 1903 and six months later in March 1904. Born in Bushton in Wiltshire around 1859, Robert was charged with being an incorrigible rogue, exposing his person. A Wesleyan by religion, Robert was sentenced to six months with hard labour and was one of the very few adults to be given twelve strokes of the birch.

James Tripp was aged thirty-four in 1902 when he was found guilty of obtaining 2s and 6d by false pretences. He was sentenced to three months in gaol with hard labour. He was a labourer from Charterhouse and a member of the Church of England.

James Stone came from Canning Town, in Essex, born there around 1875. When he was twenty-eight years old, James was photographed twice in Gloucester Gaol, once in August 1902 and again almost a year later, in August 1903. James was a groom and claimed to be of the Church of England religion. His first crime, for which he was given twelve months with hard labour, followed by three years under police supervision, was stealing a coat and a vest. Within the year he had been caught breaking into a railway station and stealing money for which he was given another twelve months in gaol with hard labour. James was known to use the alias James Walker at times.

Thirty-eight-year-old Alfred Hands was given a six-month sentence with hard labour in 1903 followed by two years under police supervision for stealing a pair of pliers, a screwdriver and a gold watch. Born in Cheshire around 1865, Alfred was a carpenter by trade.

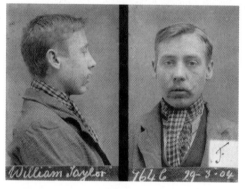

William Taylor was a twenty-three-year-old labourer from Chesterfield who was sentenced to six calendar months with hard labour for housebreaking. A member of the Church of England, William was photographed in gaol in March 1904.

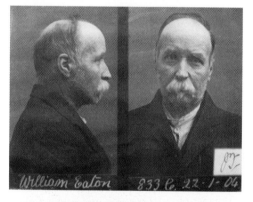

William Eaton gave Clifton on T (eme?) as his place of birth when his details were recorded in Gloucester in the first few years of the twentieth century. Photographed on 22 January 1904, William had been sentenced to eighteen months with hard labour for sheep stealing. He gave his occupation as cattle dealer and his religion as Church of England.

Originating in Cornwall, Thomas Tressiker was thirty-one when his photograph was taken in 1899. His crime was 'burglariously breaking into a dwelling house and stealing therein one gold watch, one clock and one cloth cap', for which he was given twelve months with hard labour. Thomas was a labourer and gave his religion as Church of England.

Above, from left James Clarke stated that he was born in Coventry around 1844 when he was sentenced in 1870 to two months with hard labour in Gloucester Gaol. His crime was stealing shirts. James was a single man and a fitter by trade, but was classified as a tramp at the time. He intended to go to Birmingham on his release from gaol.

Also sentenced around the same time was Charles Best. At twenty-six years old, Charles was a married painter born in Hereford. He was sentenced to six months with hard labour for stealing a knife and a brooch. When he left gaol, he planned to go to Bristol.

John Young came from Wiltshire. In 1870, when thirty years old, John was sentenced to six months in gaol with hard labour followed by three years under police supervision for stealing boots. A single man and a labourer, John was heading for Bath when he was released from prison.

Left William Dawes was a twenty-eight year old baker when he was jailed for two months with hard labour for embezzling money from his master. A single man, William stated that he was born in Wiltshire and that he intended to go to Ashton Keynes on his release.

Right John Bray was a forty-five-year-old married tailor from Manchester. In 1870 he was sentenced to four months with hard labour for stealing an umbrella. On his release from Gloucester Gaol, he intended to return to his native city.

Above, from left Henry Howard also originated from Manchester. He was forty years old when he was photographed in May 1870, found guilty of stealing a 'wrapper' and given a sentence of four months with hard labour. A groom by occupation, Henry planned to go to Cheltenham when he gained his freedom.

A third man from Manchester held in Gloucester Gaol in 1870 was John Snow. He was found guilty of stealing shirts and sentenced to one month with hard labour. A miner by occupation, John, aged thirty and unmarried, was uncertain where he would go on his release. The word 'tramp' was written on his record.

Over thirty years later, in 1902, William Thornton from Manchester was in Gloucester Gaol for stealing an overcoat. He was sentenced to fourteen days with hard labour. William was an ironworker who stated that his religion was Church of England.

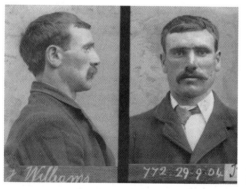

Above, from left Another inmate from Manchester was John Williams. Aged twenty-four in 1904, John was a seaman sentenced to three months with hard labour for stealing a purse and money 'from the person'. He stated that his religion was Church of England.

Walter Francis was only twenty-one years of age when he was sentenced to one month with hard labour or pay a fine of £2 13s for the 29lb of potatoes that he stole. Walter was a labourer from Danehill in Sussex who gave his religion as Church of England.

William Bartlett came from Deddington in Oxfordshire. Born around 1864, he was an inmate of Gloucester Gaol in 1904 where he was photographed on 25 November. His crime was obtaining food and lodging by false pretences, for which he was sentenced to nine months with hard labour followed by three years under police supervision. A carpenter by trade, William stated his religion was Church of England.

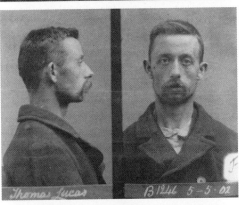

Thomas Lucas was a farm labourer from Dorhead in Wiltshire. In 1902, when aged twenty-six years, he was accused of being a rogue and a vagabond and of exposing his person. He was sentenced to six weeks of hard labour. He gave his religion as Church of England.

Aged forty-six and from Edmonton in Middlesex, George White was an inmate at Gloucester Gaol serving two calendar months with hard labour for wilfully damaging a window. George was a miner and a member of the Church of England.

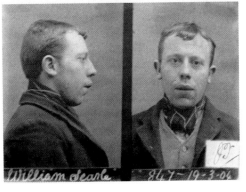

William Searle was a twenty-three-year-old jockey when he was photographed in gaol in March 1904. He had been charged with 'burglariously breaking into a dwelling house and therein stealing money and stamps'. For his crime, he was sentenced to eighteen months with hard labour. William, from Epsom in Surrey, stated that his religion was Church of England.

Above, from left George Lancaster's record states that he was born in Greverall in Wiltshire around 1865. Whatever his origins, George was in Gloucester Gaol in April 1902, having been found guilty of attempted murder and suicide for which he was given a six-month sentence. A shepherd by occupation, George recorded his religion as Church of England.

Frederick R. Mona came from Hackney. A painter by trade, he was sentenced to one month with hard labour in 1904 for stealing two pairs of boots. Frederick was forty at the time and said his religion was Church of England.

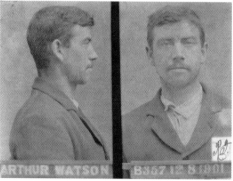

Above, from left Born in Herefordshire around 1878, Francis John Phillips was photographed twice in Gloucester Gaol, once in 1901 and again in 1902. His crime was stealing a bicycle for which he was given a sentence of nine months with hard labour. A fitter by trade, Francis was a Dissenter when it came to religion.

In 1901, Arthur Watson gave his place of birth as Hendsford in Staffordshire around 1871. Arthur was a labourer charged with stealing a bicycle. He was given a sentence of three months with hard labour for his crime. Arthur stated that his religion was Church of England.

Above, from left Ernest Spencer, aged twenty-four in 1904, gave his place of birth as Huddersfield. Ernest was sentenced to three months with hard labour for 'stealing a bicycle as a bailee'. Occasionally using the alias of Samuel Smith, Ernest had the unusual occupation of piano tuner and was of the Quaker religion.

Edward Smith was a twenty-seven-year-old bootmaker born in Islington around 1876. Edward was obviously a repeat offender as he was recorded as using aliases of Farley and Kemp. His crime in 1903 was stealing a silver watch from the person and for this he received a sentence of five years penal servitude.

Above, from left Austin Baker gave his place of birth as being Kelston in Bath but, in 1901, he found himself serving one month with hard labour in Gloucester Gaol for receiving stolen coal. Austin was the innkeeper of the Mason's Arms in Lawrence Weston near Bristol, where he lived with his wife Mary and three sons until 1923. He was forty-nine years old at the time and gave his religion as Church of England.

James Balster Uda Sampson was photographed twice in Gloucester Gaol, once in 1901 and again three years later. Born around 1861 in Milton on Thames in Kent, he was first described as a commercial traveller and then a commission agent. His first crime was obtaining 10s by false pretences. He was later accused of being an undischarged bankrupt and obtaining credit without revealing the fact. For his first offence he was given one month with hard labour and, second time round, it was increased to four months. James stated his religion was Church of England. At the time of the 1901 census, James was living as a brewer's traveller at the Rothesay Hotel in Abergavenny where his wife Mary was the licensed victualler.

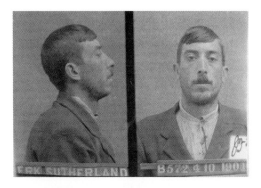

Frank Sutherland gave his birthplace as Leeds. Aged twenty-five when photographed in gaol on 4 October 1901, Frank was employed as a ship's cook. His crime, for which he was sentenced to twenty-one days with hard labour, was stealing a coat and a waistcoat. Frank said his religion was Church of England.

James Darnell came from London. Born around 1876, he was photographed twice in Gloucester Gaol, in 1903 and 1904. He was a labourer jailed for nine months with hard labour for burglary and stealing two shirts. James gave his religion as Church of England.

Born in North Shields around 1873, Edward Compton was a seaman sentenced to one calendar month with hard labour for obtaining food and lodgings by false pretences.

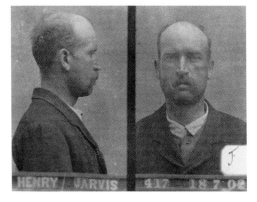

Henry Jarvis also came south, this time from Newcastle-upon-Tyne where he was born around 1860. Henry was a labourer who was sentenced to six weeks hard labour for stealing an overcoat. He stated that his religion was Church of England.

Aged forty-four in 1904, Gregory John Watts was a commission agent born in Oxford. He was sentenced to eight calendar months with hard labour for obtaining £3 7s by false pretences. Gregory stated that he was a Roman Catholic.

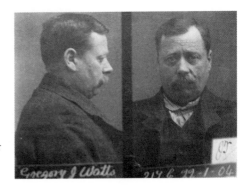

Alfred Ford was twenty-four years old when his photograph was taken in Gloucester Gaol. He gave his place of birth as Plymouth and stated that his religion was Church of England. Alfred was charged with stealing an iron boiler and four iron window frames and when he was found guilty, was sentenced to one month with hard labour.

Born in Reading around 1864, Frederick Baker was a labourer charged with stealing two pairs of boots. A member of the Church of England, Frederick was sentenced to six months with hard labour.

John Scott was a thirty-one-year-old labourer born in Richmond around 1873, who was an inmate of Gloucester Gaol in 1904. He was given a sentence of one month with hard labour for stealing a china tea service and some tools.

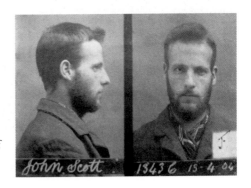

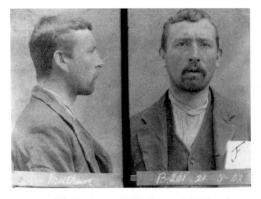

John Matthews was one of two prisoners held in Gloucester Gaol during 1902 who claimed to have been born in Salisbury. John was twenty-four years old at the time and was sentenced to twenty-one days with hard labour for stealing one ham and assaulting a man called Harry Moss. John gave his religion as being Church of England.

The other prisoner from Salisbury was forty-four-year-old Henry Stokes. Henry was a labourer and claimed he was a member of the Church of England. His crime was stealing a bag and seven chickens, for which he was given a sentence of one month with hard labour.

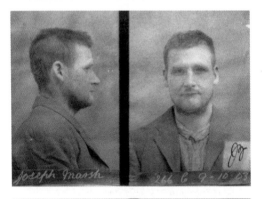

Joseph Marsh was twenty-five years old in 1903 when he was an inmate of Gloucester Gaol. Born in St Helens in Lancashire, Joseph was sentenced to four months with hard labour for stealing one sack, twenty-four glass bottles and 130lbs of rags. Although he was photographed at a different time, it seems obvious that Joseph committed his crime with John Livingstone. Joseph gave his religion as Roman Catholic.

Born in Worcester around 1880, Thomas Furber was a painter by trade. Thomas was sentenced to six weeks in gaol with hard labour for breaking into a chapel with intent to steal. Thomas, a Dissenter by religion, occasionally used the alias of John Dredge.

Richard Granger was an engineer born in West Bromwich around 1865. He was arrested for 'felony and forgery', found guilty and sentenced to six months with hard labour. Richard was a Baptist by religion.

Alfred Dobson was born in Weston-super-Mare around 1879. A photographer by trade, Alfred was given fourteen days of hard labour for obtaining food and lodgings by false pretences. A member of the Church of England, he sometimes used the alias of Ernest Seed.

Thirty-three-year-old William Day was a labourer who stated that he was born in Weymouth. He was given one calendar month with hard labour in 1901 for stealing a gun. He was a member of the Church of England.

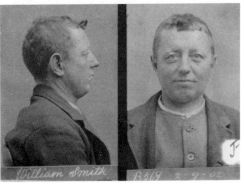

William Smith also originated in Weymouth, born there around 1866. William, a member of the Church of England, was jailed for twenty-one days for stealing a coat. He sometimes used the alias of John White.

George Butler was born in Witham in Essex around 1876. A labourer, and a member of the Church of England by religion, George was sentenced to six calendar months with hard labour for two charges of housebreaking.

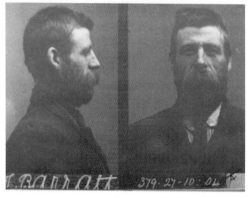

Thomas Barrett was thirty-three years old when he was photographed in Gloucester Gaol in October 1904. Thomas gave his place of birth as Wordsley and his religion as Church of England. He was given a fourteen-day sentence for housebreaking and stealing therein.

Joseph Tobin, born in York, was thirty-nine years old in 1901 when he was an inmate in Gloucester Gaol. A labourer and a Roman Catholic, Joseph stole a pair of boots and was sentenced to fourteen days with hard labour or to pay a fine of £1 15s.

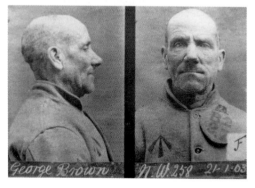

George Brown was a fifty-three-year-old stoker who gave his place of birth as Deptford. His crime was a serious one, arson, for which he was given seven years penal servitude. George stated his religion was Church of England.

Appendix A

These names are for those prisoners held in Gloucester Gaol in 1870 for whom records exist in the album but no photographs.

Thomas Aston	Oliver Dauncey	Charles Hawkes	Elizabeth Merriman	Charles Saunders
Ann Averiss	Lucy Davenport	Henry Hayes	Eliza Millard	William Scott
Henry Ayres	Edward Davis	John Hendy	John Millington	Jabez T. Scriven
Harriet Baldwin	Elizabeth Davis	John Higgs	Charles Mills	Susan Sellick
Ellen Bale	John Davis	Charles Hill	Alfred Mitchell	Eliza Shearman
James Barlow	Ruth Davis	George Hill	William Mitchell	Jane Shellard
Mary Ann Baylis	Thomas Davis	Thomas Hill	Emily Mole	Thomas Sheppard
Thomas Beard	William Davis	Harriet Hillier	Charles Morgan	Edwin Shipway
Henry Disraeli Betty	William Day	Thomas Holbrook	Sarah Morgan	William Simmonds
William Bick	Walter Deane	Harriet Holder	Oliver Mosen	Walter Sirrell
Phoebe Billingham	Edward Dixon	Heartless Holland	Mary Ann Moss	Henry Smith
Frank Bird	Benjamin Dobbs	James Howard	Ann Mott	Andrew Soul
George Bishop	William Dodd	Samuel Howells	Mary Ann Nelmes	Hannah Spencer
Mary Bond	Lydia Dyer	James Huntley	Cornelius O'Leary	Solomon Stanton
Annie Brooks	Caroline Dyke	Ralph Hurcombe	Sevan Olsen	Sarah Stephens
Caroline Brown	Eliza Edgar	William Hurcombe	George Otton	William Stephens
George Brown	Harriet Etheridge	Charlotte Hyde	Charles Paish	William Styles
John Brown	William Etheridge	William Ireland	Ann Partridge	William Sutton
William Brown	Walter Fisher	Francis Jackson	Walter Partridge	Ephraim Taylor
Albert Bruton	Alfred Floyd	Richard Jackson	James Payne	Henry Thomas
Henry Burford	Thomas Fricker	James Jarvis	Manfred Phelps	John Thompson
William Cake	John Frith	John Jones	James Phillips	Charles Thurney
Joseph Carter	William Gardner	Sarah Jordan	Sarah Pinchin	Richard Tiley
Thomas Chandler	George Gibbs	Clement Kidwell	James Pollard	Mary Tilling
John Cherrington	Charles Henry Gingell	James Kingdom	Thomas Powell	Ellen Tipper
Thomas Church	Joseph Gingell	Charles Lang	Henry Pready	Charlotte Verrier
William Clayton	Joseph Golding	Robert Law	William Pritchard	Charles Vicks
Emma Ada Clifford	Thomas Goodwin	William Lloyd	George Pyser	Joseph Waine
George Clutterbuck	James Grant	Charles Lodge	George Rayner	Alfred John Walker
Charles Collett	William Green	James Lovesy	Ellen Reeks	Robert Wallbridge
John Collingbourne	Ellen Griffin	Charles Low	Ann Rees	Mary Ann Watkins
Charles Cook	Jane Griffin	Edward Lusty	James Roach	George White
Alfred Cooke	Hannah Gwilliam	Andrew Marini	John Robbins	Samuel White
Annie Critchley	Henry Haines	Charles Marshall	Mary Ann Roberts	John Wicks
Fanny Croaker	Thomas Haines	Daniel Martin	Rosina Roberts	Mary Wilkes
James Croaker	William E.F. Hall	Mary May	George Rummins	David Williams
Sarah Cummings	Edward Hankwright	Henry Merchant	William Sargeant	John Williams

Mary Williams
Thomas Williams
Richard Williford
Charles Willis junior

Elizabeth Wilson
Emma Wilson
Walter Wilson
John Wiltshire

Delina Windows
Thomas Wood
George Wookey
Rufus Workman

Margaret Yeates

APPENDIX B

These are the names of the prisoners for whom photographs exist in the albums but which have not been included in the book.

Elizabeth Alcock
John Alexander
Charles Allen
James Allen
Joseph Appleby
John Armstrong
Henry Atkins
John Bailey
John Baker
Henry Banks
Michael Barlow
John Barrett
Aaron Bates
George Baylis
Charles Beal
William Bearcroft
Charles Beard
James Bedford
George Bennett
Sarah Ann Berry
William Berry
Reuben Billington
Richard Bird
Samuel Bishop
Frederick Boden
Frank Bonnick
Charles Firth Booth
James Bosworth
Edwin Bowen
Thomas Bowles
George Bracher
William H. Bradshaw

William Brewer
John Bright
Harry Brooks
Joseph Brooks
George Brown
Patrick Brown
Thomas Brown
John Burnett
Arthur Burrington
Henry Butcher
John Caflin
Henry Charlton
William Christie
Arthur Churnside
Benjamin Clarke
Henry Clarke
William Clarke
Ambrose Cook
John Cook
Thomas Cooke
Edward Cooper
George Cooper
Richard Cooper
William Cotterell
George Cox
James Cox
Thomas Cox
George Crew
Henry Curtis
William Curtis
Henry Dancey
George Davies

Henry Davies
Leonard Davies
Samuel Davies
Thomas Davies
William Davies
Florence Davis
William Davis
Charles Dickenson
James Digweed
Alfred Dix
James Dodd
William Doorham
John Downes
Frank Durham
Ames Edmonds
William Edwards
John Elton
William England
Charles Evans
George Evans
Leonard Evans
Robert Evans
Thomas Evans
Arthur Farmer
James Fegan
Thomas Fletcher
John Morris Flynn
James Follows
James Fox
Thomas Fox
Herbert Frost
Patrick Furey

William Garbett
William Henry Garret
Cyprus Giles
George Grenadier Gill
Matthew Goodden
Alfred T. Gough
Alfred Gough
Stephen Goulding
John Greenwood
Alfred Griswood
William Gundy
Ernest Haines
John Hall
John Hallam
Hudson Handford
George Harper
Alfred Harris
Edwin Harris
George Harris
John Harris
William Harris
Charles Harrison
John Francis Hartland
John Harvey
William Hatton
Thomas F. Hayward
Charles Hemmings
Henry Herbert
Frederick Hewlett
Robert Higginbottom
William Higgins
William C. Higgins

Thomas Hill
William Hinton
William E. Hirons
Edwin Hodnett
Samuel Holder
Frederick Hollinshead
Annie Holloway
John Holloway
Thomas Holloway
Thomas Hopley
James Hopson
William Horn
Thomas Hughes
Walter Hughes
William Ireland
James Jackson
Thomas Jenkins
William Jenkins
William Jeynes
Samuel Johns
Henry Johnson
John Johnson
William Johnson
William H. Johnson
Albert Jones
Alfred Jones
Annie Jones
Arthur Jones
Charles Jones
Elizabeth Jones
George Jones
Henry Jones

James Jones
James L. Jones
John Jones
Pryce Jones
Thomas Jones
William Jones
John Jordan
William Henry Jubb
Frederick W. Kent
Robert Key
George King
John Kinsman
Frederick J. Lakin
George W. Lander
Frederick Lane
George Lawson
Thomas Lea
Herod Lediard
William Lee
William Leonard
Alfred Weyman Lewis
Charles Henry Lewis
Richard Lewis
Thomas Lewis
William Lewis
Albert E. Limbrick
Edward Lloyd
George Lloyd
George Richard Lloyd
Robert Long
Elijah Loud
Frederick Lowrie
Alexander Mackay
Robert Mackenzie
John Macklin
Hugh John Maguire
James T. Maloney
John Mansell
John Mapp
George J Mapps
Charles Martin
John Matthews
Robert McKenzie

William H. McKinder
James McLean
Austin McSheedy
Frederick Medlicott
Stephen Memory
Daniel Merchant
John Merriday
William Miles
Archibald Miller
Henry Millwood
Edward Milton
William Minton
Samuel Mitchell
Walter Mitchell
William Mitchell
William Mole
Godfrey Morgan
John Morgan
Oliver Morgan
Charles Morris
Henry Morris
Thomas Morris
Walter Morris
James Moynihan
Thomas Nash
William Noble
James Oliver
Michael O'Neill
John O'Niel
James Orpwood
Francis Osborne
John Osborne
Benjamin Owen
Frederick William
John Owen
Harry Page
William Palmer
Christopher Parr
Samuel Parry
James Parsons
Stephen Parsons
George Passey
George Pearce

John Pearce
Alfred Pennington
John Penry
Ernest Perks
Thomas Phillips
William Phillips
Arthur Pitcher
Arthur Poole
George Powell
Thomas Joseph Powell
Alfred Preece
Charles Preedy
Albert Presbury
Charles Price
Francis Price
Frank Price
John Price
William Prince
Charles H. Probert
William Prosser
Herbert E. Quainton
James Read
John Reidy
Robert Riley
William Roberts
John Robinson
Christopher Rogers
James Ross
Henry Rosser
Samuel Rowe
Sidney Rudge
Thomas Rutter
Thomas Ryan
William Sadler
Henry Sage
William Sandall
John Saunders
George Selby
Henry Sherrington
Moses Shiels
William Shinn
William Shovell
Thomas Simson

Jason Skerrett
George Smallman
Charles Smith
Frederick Smith
Henry Smith
John Smith
Philip Smith
Richard Smith
Samuel Smith
Sidney Smith
Thomas Smith
William Smith
Richard Spiers
Arthur Stephens
C. Sterry
Weston Stratton
John Sullivan
William Swann
Alfred Symonds
James Taft
Albert Taylor
Andrew Taylor
Henry Taylor
James Taylor
John Taylor
William Tetsell
Arthur Thomas
George H. Thomas
Edward Thompson
Robert Thorn
Edward Thornhill
Frank Thornton
George Tilton
Henry Tudor
John Turner
John Underwood
John A. Vaughan
Joseph Vaughan
Thomas Vaughan
William Vaughan
Gerald Vincent
George Wainwright
William Henry Waites

Frederick Walker
Francis Wall
William Wall
John Walsh
Amos Walton
Mary Ward
Henry Warner
George Watkins
Edwin Watson
Harry Watson
Thomas Webb
John Welsh
Alfred Went
Samuel West
Henry Wheeler
Alfred White
George White
Thomas White
Alfred Williams
Charles Williams
David Williams
Frederick Williams
George Williams
Henry Williams
John Williams
Morris Williams
Thomas Williams
William D. Williams
George Wilson
John Windsor
Walter Winstone
John Withers
Arthur Edwin Wood
William Wood
James Woodhouse
George F. Worgan
Arthur Wright
Francis Wynde

Appendix C

This database includes all known details of the prisoners mentioned and/or photographed in the three albums Q/Gc/10/1, Q/Gc/10/2 and Q/Gc/10/4, which are held at Gloucestershire Archives.

Album	Sex	Surname	Forenames	Ref. No.	Age	Date of Photo	Birthplace	Marital	Occupation	Offence	Sentence	Destination	Religion	Notes
2	F	ALCOCK	Elizabeth	12		04/07/1891								
2	F	ALCOCKS	Elizabeth	3		18/07/1888								
4	M	ALEXANDER	John	611	22	29/11/1904	Not known		Labourer	Shopbreaking and stealing therein after PCF	2 months HL		RC	
2	M	ALLEN	Charles	17		28/12/1891								
2	M	ALLEN	James	CJW1556		2/11/04								Same man as James SMITH 40/3. Allan in index
4	M	AMES	William	64	47	25/11/1904	Bournemouth		Sailor	Obtaining charitable contributions under false pretences	6 months HL & 2yrs PS		Wesleyan	
4	M	ANDREWS	Edward George	C801	25	29/03/1904	Cheltenham		Fishmonger	Stealing timber, tools, etc	6 cal months HL		CoE	
4	M	ANDREWS	Robert	B296	34	02/08/1901	Gloucester		Fitter	Stealing a bag and £26 from the Midland Railway Co	6 weeks HL		CoE	
4	M	APPLEBY	Joseph	A438		25/09/1900								
2	M	ARCHER	Thomas	392		1/21/01								
2	M	ARMSTRONG	John	270		04/04/1891								
1	M	ASTON	Thomas	147	26	03/05/1870	Blakeney	M	Collier	Stealing money	1y Hard Labour	Blakeney		
4	M	ATKINS	Henry	TX37		07/07/1902								
1	F	AVERISS	Ann	82	23	30/01/1870	Winchcombe	M	Charwoman	Stealing bed linen, etc.	1m Hard Labour	Cheltenham		
1	M	AYRES	Henry	186	18	06/05/1870	Wotton under Edge	S	Labourer	Stealing a watch	6m Hard Labour	Colesbourne		
2	M	BAILEY	John	176		10/30/05								
1	F	BAILEY	Sarah Ann	239	39	04/06/1870	Hasfield	M	None	Stealing dress stuff	1m Hard Labour	Harescombe		
4	M	BAKER	Austin	B209	49	10/07/1910	Kelston, Bath		Innkeeper	Receiving stolen coal	1 month HL		CoE	
4	M	BAKER	Frederick	C186	39	03/12/1903	Reading		Labourer	Stealing 2 pairs of boots	6 months HL		CoE	

Album	Sex	Surname	Forenames	Ref. No.	Age	Date of Photo	Birthplace	Marital	Occupation	Offence	Sentence	Destination	Religion	Notes
4	M	BAKER	John	A397		01/11/1899				Stealing earings (sic)	2m Hard Labour	Gloucester		
1	F	BALDWIN	Harriet	50	17	30/04/1870	Gloucester	S	Servant	Stealing money	1m Hard Labour	Cirencester		
1	F	BALE	Ellen	65	15	30/04/1870	Cirencester	S	Servant					Photo removed
2	M	BANKS	Henry	576		01/12/1894								
4	M	BARKER	William	104	20	19/09/1904	Oldham		Sailor	Burglary & Office breaking	4 months HL		CoE	
Album	Sex	Surname	Forenames	Ref. No.	Age	Date of Photo	Birthplace	Marital	Occupation	Offence	Sentence	Destination	Religion	Notes
1	M	BARLOW	James	149	21	03/05/1870	Hull	S	Tramp	Stealing a candlestick	1y Hard Labour	Uncertain		
2	M	BARLOW	Michael	186										
4	M	BARNES	William	B198	48	21/05/1902	Southampton		Labourer	Stealing one ham	21 days HL		CoE	
2	F	BARRETT	Jane	91		12/18/02								
2	M	BARRETT	John	558		3/20/03								
4	M	BARRETT	Thomas	379	33	27/10/1904	Wordsley		Labourer	Shopbreaking and stealing therein after PCF	14 days HL		CoE	
4	M	BARTLETT	William	1479	40	25/11/1904	Deddington		Carpenter	False pretences – food and lodging	9 months HL & 3yrs PS		CoE	
2	M	BARTON	Grant	X51		3/25/02								
2	M	BATES	Aaron	200		10/13/03								
2	M	BAYLIS	George	2542		21/04/1883								BAYLISS
1	F	BAYLIS	Mary Ann	15	20	30/04/1870	Kempley	S	Servant	Cheat	9m Hard Labour	Gloucester		
2	M	BEAL	Charles	620		6/25/06								or BEALE
2	M	BEARCROFT	William	664		7/17/06								
2	M	BEARD	Charles	112		9/10/03								
1	M	BEARD	Thomas	68	17	30/04/1870	Stroud	S	Labourer	Stealing wearing apparel	4m Hard Labour	Stroud		
2	M	BEDFORD	James	22		24/10/1885								
2	M	BENNETT	George	319		9/25/1900								
2	F	BERRY	Sarah Ann											See STOREY
2	M	BERRY	William	750		3/17/05								
1	M	BEST	Charles	258	26	18/06/1870	Hereford	M	Painter	Stealing knife & brooch	6w Hard Labour	Bristol		
1	M	BETTY	Henry Disraeli	141	16	03/05/1870	Kingswood	S	Butcher	Stealing money	6w Hard Labour	Kingswood nr Bristol		
1	M	BICK	William	101	14	29/04/1870	Grange Court, GLS	S	Labourer	Stealing butter	1m Hard Labour	Westbury on Severn		
4	M	BICKNELL	Arthur	C768	28	18/09/1903	Leamington		Stoker	Stealing PO bank book, 2 bank pass books, cheque book & one cash box	12 cal months HL		CoE	Alias Arthur HARRIS
4	M	BIGWOOD	Henry	87	46	14/11/1904	Warmley		Labourer	Stealing 4s 6d in money after PCF	5 months HL & 2yrs PS		CoE	

Album	Surname	Forenames	Ref.No.	Age	Date of Photo	Birthplace	Sex	Marital	Occupation	Offence	Sentence	Destination	Religion	Notes
4	BIGWOOD	Henry	A9	55	25/04/1900	Eldersfield	M		Charwoman	Stealing coal	2m Hard Labour	Newnham		
1	BILLINGHAM	Phoebe	195		06/05/1870		F							
2	BILLINGTON	Reuben William	284		12/18/02		M							
1	BIRD	Frank	172	12	03/05/1870	Somerset	M	S	Labourer	Stealing newspapers	20d Imprisonment & 4y R	Gloucester		
2	BIRD	Richard	694		10/16/06		M							
1	BISHOP	George	91	18	28/04/1870	Cirencester	M	S	Factory Hand	Stealing hay	3m Hard Labour	Chalford		
2	BISHOP	Samuel	250		14/07/1894		M							
4	BODEN	Frederick	A405		05/02/1900		M							
1	BOND	Mary	16	17	30/04/1870	Gloucester	F	S	Book binder	Stealing money	9m Hard Labour	Gloucester		
1	BOND	Walter	265	16	25/06/1870	Charlton Kings	M	S	Labourer	Stealing Fowls	3m Hard Labour	Charlton Kings		
4	BOND	William	C113	48	30/04/1904	Cinderford	M		Clock repairer	Obtaining a watch by false pretences	12 cal months HL		CoE	Alias SMITH & HILL
2	BONNICK	Frank	638		7/6/06		M							Page 37
2	BOOTEN	Thomas	563		8/24/04		M							BOOTON?
2	BOOTH	Charles Firth					M							
4	BOSWORTH	James	C222	38	09/09/1903	[Blank]	M		Insurance Agent	Stealing £1 7s and 8s 9d	3 cal months HL		CoE	
2	BOTCHETT	Russell	564		12/9/02		M							
4	BOWEN	Edwin	A287		05/02/1900		M							
4	BOWLES	Thomas	B1217	26	21/03/1902	London	M		Labourer	Stealing one pair of boots	1 month HL		CoE	
2	BRACHER	George	419		1/21/01		M							
2	BRADSHAW	William Henry	164		13/04/1889		M							See Garrett
1	BRAIN	Frederick	280	24	02/07/1870	Swindon	M	M	Labourer	Stealing a Grindstone	14d Hard Labour	Gloucester		
1	BRAY	John	212	45	06/05/1870	Manchester	M	S	Tailor	Stealing umbrella	4m Hard Labour	Manchester		
2	BREWER	William	558	62	08/05/1896	Painswick	M		Plasterer	Attempted suicide	10 days HL		CoE	
4	BRIDGES	George	B510		21/10/1901		M							
2	BRIGHT	John	90		11/8/05		M							
1	BRITTON	Sarah	236	20	28/05/1870	Hanham	F	S	Servant	Stealing watch	3m Hard Labour	Bristol		
1	BROOKS	Annie	21	13	30/05/1870	Cheltenham	F	S	Labourer	Stealing money	14d Hard Labour	Cheltenham		
4	BROOKS	Harry	R35		12/03/1891		M							
4	BROOKS	Joseph	A82		03/10/1900		M							
4	BROOKS	Joseph S	A57		30/08/1899		M							
4	BROWN	Annie	B132	28	07/11/1901	Cheltenham	F		Prostitute	Stealing 2s 6d	5 months HL		CoE	
1	BROWN	Caroline	88	40	28/04/1870	Upton St Leonards	F	M	Labourer	Stealing potatoes	14d Hard Labour	Stonehouse		
1	BROWN	George	122	17	29/04/1870	Painswick	M	S	Labourer	Stealing fowls	2m Hard Labour	Painswick		
4	BROWN	George	NW258	53	21/01/1903	Deptford	M		Stoker	Arson	7 years PS		CoE	
2	BROWN	George	CXS848		27/07/1892		M							

Album	Sex	Surname	Forenames	Ref. No.	Age	Date of Photo	Birthplace	Marital	Occupation	Offence	Sentence	Destination	Religion	Notes	Schoolhouse
4	F	BROWN	Julia	A286		26/07/1900									
4	F	BROWN	Kate	A97		30/08/1899									
2	M	BROWN	Patrick											See Morgan Page 10	
4	M	BROWN	Thomas	A272		29/11/1899									
1	M	BROWN	William	120	18	30/04/1870	Kingswood	S	Labourer	Stealing money	10d Hard Labour	Kingswood			
1	M	BRUTON	Albert	127	20	29/04/1870	Kingswood	S	Weaver	Stealing sweets	10d Imprisonment	Kingswood			
1	M	BURFORD	Henry	73	35	30/04/1870	Stroud	M	Brewer	Stealing beer	7d Hard Labour	Gloucester			
2	M	BURNETT	John	376		02/07/1887									
2	M	BURRINGTON	Arthur											Or POOLE	
2	M	BURTON	James	455		04/04/1887									
2	M	BURTON	Joseph	282		3/25/02									
2	M	BUTCHER	Henry	424		15/10/1885									
4	M	BUTLER	George	B1138	26	25/09/1903	Witham, ESS		Labourer	Housebreaking - 2 charges	6 cal months HL		CoE		
2	M	CAFLIN	John	731		3/17/05									See FUREY	
1	M	CAKE	William	106	47	30/04/1870	Dorset	M	Labourer	Stealing wood	1m Hard Labour	Thornbury			
4	M	CALLAGHAN	Stephen	B1012	32	31/01/1902	London		Labourer	Stealing 2 pairs of boots	14 days HL		RC	Page 7 missing	
4	M	CANTER	Albert	A620	27	18/03/1902	Ireland		Labourer	Stealing 2 dozen glass tumblers	6 months HL		RC	Alias Michael FEINEY and Thomas ARNETT	
1	M	CARTER	Joseph	140	22	29/04/1870	Gloucester	M	Labourer	Stealing a cap	20d Hard Labour	Gloucester			
2	M	CASTREE	Charles	4403		30/06/1885									
2	M	CASTREE	David											See George POWELL Page 5	
2	M	CASTREE	Edwin	343		30/06/1894									
2	M	CASTREE	George	4061		01/07/1884									
2	M	CASTREE	George	375		02/04/1887									
2	M	CASTREE	James	2748		15/10/1883									
2	M	CASTREE	James	G8996		26/08/1889									
2	M	CASTREE	Jeremiah	4402		30/09/1884									
2	M	CASTREE	William	345		27/02/1889									
2	F	CHANDLER	Elizabeth	4155		01/10/1883									
2	F	CHANDLER	Elizabeth	4505		04/10/1884									
2	M	CHANDLER	George	174		18/01/1892									
2	M	CHANDLER	George	610		13/04/1895									
2	M	CHANDLER	James	H892		26/08/1889									
2	M	CHANDLER	James	106		31/12/1895									
1	M	CHANDLER	Thomas	162	36	03/05/1870	Coleford	M	Collier	Stealing cider	14d Hard Labour	Coleford			

Album	Sex	Surname	Forenames	Ref. No.	Age	Date of Photo	Birthplace	Marital	Occupation	Offence	Sentence	Destination	Religion	Notes
2	F	CHAPPEL	Harriet Agnes	4		18/07/1888								
4	M	CHAPPLE	Alfred	B507	22	28/09/1901	London		Seaman	Stealing 2 rugs and one shirt	14 days HL		CoE	See BUTCHER. Page 4
2	M	CHARLTON	Henry											
1	M	CHERRINGTON	John	104	32	30/04/1870	Gloucester	S	Labourer	Stealing a coat	20d Hard Labour	Gloucester		
2	M	CHRISTY	William	333		03/11/1886								
1	M	CHURCH	Thomas	38	31	30/04/1870	Quenington	S	Labourer	Stealing a horse skin	18m Hard Labour	Quenington		
Album	Sex	Surname	Forenames	Ref. No.	Age	Date of Photo	Birthplace	Marital	Occupation	Offence	Sentence	Destination	Religion	Notes
2	M	CHURNSIDE	Arthur	334		9/2/02								
4	M	CLARE	John	B225	62	23/05/1902	Huntingdon		Carpenter	Stealing carpenter's tools	1 month HL		CoE	Alias Samuel SAINT
2	M	CLARKE	Benjamin	304		12/05/1898								
2	M	CLARKE	Henry											Or WHEELER. Page 42
1	M	CLARKE	James	219	26	07/05/1870	Coventry	S	Fitter (Tramp)	Stealing shirts	2m Hard Labour	Birmingham		
2	F	CLARKE	Lucy	149		26/07/1897								
2	M	CLARKE	Thomas	494		30/06/1898								
2	M	CLARKE	William	149		17/01/1888								
1	M	CLAYTON	William	92	40	28/04/1870	Wales	S	Labourer	Stealing timber	7d Hard Labour	West Dean		
4	M	CLEMENTS	George	B188	79	06/09/1901	Arlingham		Boatman	Stealing food and clothing from a vessel	3 months HL		CoE	
1	M	CLEMENTS	Nathaniel	213	33	07/05/1870	[Blank]	[Blank]	Stonemason	Stealing meal?	1m Hard Labour	Rodborough		
1	F	CLIFFORD	Emma Ada	185	14	03/05/1870	Gloucester	S	Factory Hand	Stealing books	14d Hard Labour & 5y R	Gloucester		
1	M	CLUTTERBUCK	George	56	57	30/04/1870	Norton	S	Labourer	Stealing coal	1m Hard Labour	Cheltenham		
2	F	COFFEE	Mary	45		18/02/1893								
2	M	COLE	George	520		3/20/03								
1	M	COLEMAN	George	217	20	07/05/1870	Herefordshire	S	Labourer	Stealing rabbit trap	1m Hard Labour	Newent		
4	M	COLEMAN	John	418	62	18/07/1902	Ireland		Labourer	Stealing lady's jacket	21 days HL		CoE	
4	M	COLLETT	Charles	72	18	30/04/1870	Tewkesbury	S	Factory Hand	Stealing a box	2d imprisonment	Tewkesbury		
1	M	COLLETT	John	178	24	03/05/1870	Cheltenham	S	Servant	Stealing coats	3m Hard Labour	Cheltenham		
4	M	COMPTON	Edward	B103	28	03/06/1901	N.Shields	S	Seaman	Obtaining food and lodgings by false pretences	1 Cal. Month HL		CoE	
2	M	COOK	Ambrose	S377		08/11/1892								S/377
1	M	COOK	Charles	94	23	28/04/1870	Dunsbourne	M	Woodman	Cheat	18m Hard Labour	Dunsbourne		Very bad character'
2	M	COOK	John	57		11/07/1894								
1	M	COOKE	Alfred	187	27	06/05/1870	Cheltenham	M	Labourer	Stealing fowls	6m Hard Labour	Cheltenham		
2	F	COOKE	Sarah Ann	35		16/07/1889								

Album	Sex	Surname	Forenames	Ref. No.	Age	Date of Photo	Birthplace	Marital	Occupation	Offence	Sentence	Destination	Religion	Notes
2	M	COOKE	Thomas	90		12/04/1893								
4	M	COOPER	Edward	A945		15/06/1899								
2	M	COOPER	George	341		1/23/03								Or WELSH
1	M	COOPER	John	225	48	14/05/1870	Thornbury	S	Labourer	Stealing hayknife	1m Hard Labour	NFA – uncertain		
2	M	COOPER	Richard	457		12/9/02								
1	M	COOPER	William	247	48	11/06/1870	Littledean	M	Collier	Stealing hay	1m Hard Labour	East Dean		
2	M	COTTERELL	William	347		21/10/1886								
2	M	COTTERELL	William	66		15/07/1892								
4	M	COUNSELL	Alfred	B647	48	23/10/1901	Bristol		Labourer	Stealing a pair of boots	1 Cal month HL		CoE	
4	M	COURT	George	B693	46	03/10/1902	Newnham		Blacksmith	Breaking into a blacksmith's shop and stealing therein 1 file, 1 hammer, etc.	4 weeks HL		CoE	
Album	Sex	Surname	Forenames	Ref. No.	Age	Date of Photo	Birthplace	Marital	Occupation	Offence	Sentence	Destination	Religion	Notes
4	M	COX	Frederick Charles	C1362	30	05/05/1904	Cheltenham		Labourer	Stealing lead	6 weeks HL		CoE	
1	M	COX	George	242	32	04/06/1870	Cam	S	Plasterer	Arson – shed	18m Hard Labour	Cam		
4	M	COX	George	A718		22/01/1900								
2	M	COX	James	Q194		19/07/1890								Q/194
4	M	COX	James Thomas	B349	28	10/12/1902	Kemble		Labourer	Maliciously throwing stones at a railway carriage	6 months HL		CoE	
4	M	COX	Thomas	B652	41	12/08/1902	Tetbury		Labourer	Incorrigible rogue	12 cal months HL		CoE	
Album	Sex	Surname	Forenames	Ref. No.	Age	Date of Photo	Birthplace	Marital	Occupation	Offence	Sentence	Destination	Religion	Notes
4	M	COX	Thomas	C417	48	04/01/1904	Tetbury		Labourer	Exposing his person; incorrigible rogue	3 cal months HL		CoE	
2	M	COX	Thomas	A312		22/11/1900								
2	M	CREW	George	259		04/07/1892								
1	F	CRITCHLEY	Annie	62	14	30/04/1870	Cheltenham	S	Servant	Cheat	10d Hard Labour	Cheltenham		
1	F	CROAKER	Fanny	76	37	30/04/1870	Painswick	S	Field Labourer	Stealing bread	7d Hard Labour	Cheltenham		
1	M	CROAKER	James	93	26	28/04/1870	Bristol	M	Labourer	Uttering counterfeit coin	18m Hard Labour	Thornbury		
1	F	CROWDER	Elizabeth	229	14	14/05/1870	Cheltenham	S	Servant	Stealing purse & other items	7d Hard Labour	Cheltenham		
4	M	CROXSON	Alfred Bell	421	40	14/11/1904	Toronto		Clerk	Larceny after PCF	6 weeks HL		CoE	Alias Walter RICHARDS
2	M	CROXSON	Alfred Bell	852		8/23/05								Or COTSON?
4	M	CULABINE	Ernest	A307		14/08/1900								
1	F	CUMMINGS	Sarah	204	37	06/05/1870	Cheltenham	M	Cook	Stealing meat & flour	14d Hard Labour	Cheltenham		
4	M	CUNNINGHAM	Josiah	B11	36	23/06/1902	America		Corn Porter	Stealing 3 ropes, 124 lbs of iron bolts & 71 lbs of nails	3 cal months HL		CoE	
2	M	CURTIS	Henry	782		09/07/1896								

Album	Sex	Surname	Forenames	Ref. No.	Age	Date of Photo	Birthplace	Marital	Occupation	Offence	Sentence	Destination	Religion	Notes
4	M	CURTIS	William	B135	62	06/05/1902	Ledworth, WIL		Labourer	Stealing 10 half crowns	21 days HL		CoE	Same as William Cotterell?
2	M	CURTIS	William	168		14/04/1894								
2	M	CURTIS	William											Page 17?
4	M	DALLIMORE	William	C1011	21	16/07/1903	Bath		Soldier	Burglariously breaking into a dwelling house and therein stealing one clock	6 months HL		CoE	
4	M	DANCEY	Henry	A30		03/10/1900								
4	F	DARNELL	Frances	C170	25	10/02/1904	lincolnshire		None	Burglary & stealing 2 shirts	9 cal months HL		RC	
4	M	DARNELL	James	C169	27	15/05/1903	London		Labourer	Burglary and stealing two shirts, etc.	9 cal months HL		CoE	
Album	Sex	Surname	Forenames	Ref. No.	Age	Date of Photo	Birthplace	Marital	Occupation	Offence	Sentence	Destination	Religion	Notes
4	M	DARNELL	James	169	27	10/02/1904	London		Labourer	Burglary & stealing 2 shirts	9 cal months HL		CoE	
1	M	DAUNCEY	Oliver	135	24	29/05/1870	Eastington	M	Carpenter	Stealing tools	8m Hard Labour	Stroud		
1	F	DAVENPORT	Lucy	35	32	30/04/1870	Preston	M	Tramp	Stealing a jacket	7d Hard Labour	Uncertain		
2	F	DAVIES	Elizabeth	108		3/3/03								
2	M	DAVIES	George	126		31/08/1886								
2	M	DAVIES	George	WCK48		05/04/1892								w.c.k.48
2	M	DAVIES	Henry	178		8/24/1900								
2	M	DAVIES	John	540		3/20/03								
2	M	DAVIES	Joseph	302		9/2/02								
2	M	DAVIES	Leonard	343		02/12/1893								
2	M	DAVIES	Percy	483		10/22/1900								
2	M	DAVIES	Samuel	356		26/07/1889								
2	M	DAVIES	Thomas	FS931		27/07/1892								F.S.931
2	M	DAVIES	William	Co619		29/10/1888								
1	M	DAVIS	Edward	150	16	03/05/1870	Cheltenham	S	Labourer	Stealing wearing apparel	1y Hard Labour	Cheltenham		
1	F	DAVIS	Elizabeth	79	27	30/04/1870	Kingstanley	M	None	Stealing books	1m Hard Labour	Painswick		
2	F	DAVIS	Florence											Alias KENNEDY
4	M	DAVIS	George	B624	45	10/21/01	Bristol	S	Hawker	Stealing 7 pairs of socks	1 Cal month HL	Cheltenham	CoE	
1	M	DAVIS	John	42	57	30/04/1870	Bath	S	Painter	Unlawfully wounding	9m Hard Labour	Cheltenham		
1	F	DAVIS	Ruth	190	20	06/05/1870	Wickwar	S	Dressmaker	Cheat	1m Hard Labour	Wotton under Edge		
1	M	DAVIES	Thomas	193	44	06/05/1870	Lydney	S	Seaman	Stealing fowls	3m Hard Labour	Uncertain		
1	M	DAVIS	William	111	23	30/04/1870	Hereford	S	Boatman	Stealing a coat	2m Hard Labour	Gloucester		
2	M	DAVIS	Wm.	4135		01/01/1885								
1	M	DAWES	William	230	28	21/05/1870	Wilts	S	Baker	Embezzling money from master	2m Hard Labour	Ashton Keynes		
4	M	DAWSON	Thomas	B543	36	10/7/01	Ireland		Labourer	Being in the outhouse with intent to steal fowl	7 days HL		RC	Photo loose. Alias Thomas DALTON
1	M	DAY	William	54	17	30/04/1870	Ampney Crucis	S	Labourer	Stealing gin	1m Hard Labour	Ampney Crucis		
4	M	DAY	William	B586	33	10/7/01	Weymouth		Labourer	Stealing a gun	1 Cal month HL		CoE	

Album	Sex	Surname	Forenames	Ref. No.	Age	Date of Photo	Birthplace	Marital	Occupation	Offence	Sentence	Destination	Religion	Notes
1	M	DEE	Charles	260	20	25/06/1870	Avening	M	Labourer	Stealing an axe	12m Hard Labour	Painswick		Apprehended Rodborough?
2	M	DELAVOUS	Louis	107		27/03/1886								DELAVO?
2	M	DICKENSON	Charles	1049		24/09/1897								Or DICKINSON
2	M	DIGWEED	James	203		10/19/01								Not in index under D
1	M	DIX	Alfred	244		25/06/1870	Mangotsfield		Labourer	Stealing money	14d	Fishponds		
1	M	DIXON	Edward	34	14	30/04/1870	Coleford	S		Stealing oats	3m Hard Labour	Coleford		
1	M	DOBBS	Benjamin	201	29	06/05/1870	Coleford	M	Hawker	Obtaining food and lodging by false pretences	14 days HL		CoE	Alias Ernest SEED
4	M	DOBSON	Alfred	B271	22	7/25/01	Weston super Mare	M	Photographer					
2	M	DODD	James	282		29/12/1890								Or DOBBINS
1	M	DODD	William	13	19	30/04/1870	Bath	S	Cutler	Stealing grinding machine	2m Hard Labour	Uncertain		
2	M	DOORHAM	William Frederick	474		7/28/03								
2	M	DOWNES	John	622		20/10/1898								
4	M	DUFFETY	Dennis	B1062	50	3/18/02	Bristol		Labourer	Stealing 64 lbs of hay	6 weeks HL		CoE	
4	M	DUFFETY	Gilbert	B1063	19	3/18/02	Henbury, Bristol		Mop & skewer maker	Stealing 64 lbs of hay	6 weeks HL		CoE	
4	M	DUFFETY	Gilbert	B10		7/10/01								
2	M	DURHAM	Frank											Alias William Frederick Doorham?
1	F	DYER	Lydia	105	17	30/04/1870	Yate	S	Servant	Stealing wearing apparel	3m Hard Labour	Yate		
1	F	DYKE	Caroline	12	19	30/04/1870	Cheltenham	S	Unemployed	Stealing bread	7d Hard Labour	Cheltenham		
1	F	DYKE	Emma	278	19	02/07/1870	Cheltenham	S	Unemployed	Stealing Money	6m Hard Labour & 7y Police Supervision	Cheltenham		
4	M	EATON	William	C833	56	1/22/04	Clifton on T	S	Cattle dealer	Sheep Stealing	18 months HL		CoE	
1	F	EDGAR	Eliza	89	36	28/04/1870	Glastonbury	M	Servant	Stealing a shirt	3m Hard Labour	Bristol		
2	M	EDMONDS	James	102		14/01/1888								
1	M	EDWARDS	John	224	66	07/05/1870	Chester	S	Clerk (Tramp)	Burglary	9m Hard Labour	Liverpool		Alias Craig
4	M	EDWARDS	Richard	B582	75	8/12/02	Bisley		Butcher	Shooting with intent and found guilty of grievous bodily harm	11 months HL		CoE	
2	M	EDWARDS	William	185		18/04/1893								
2	M	ELTON	John											Alias Thomas JONES?
2	M	ENGLAND	William	439		01/05/1889								
1	M	ESSEX	John	243	21	04/06/1870	Rodborough	S	Labourer	Robbery with Violence	18m Hard Labour	Houndscroft nr Stroud		
1	F	ETHERIDGE	Harriet	86	37	30/04/1870	Newnham	M	Washer	Stealing wearing apparel	7m Hard Labour	Newnham		
1	M	ETHERIDGE	William	27	18	30/04/1870	Oxley, GLS	S	Labourer	Stealing a scarf	1m Hard Labour	Longhope		

Album	Sex	Surname	Forenames	Ref. No.	Age	Date of Photo	Birthplace	Marital	Occupation	Offence	Sentence	Destination	Religion	Notes
2	M	EVANS	Charles	607		6/25/06								Vide LLOYD
2	M	EVANS	George	279		29/06/1891								Or A' Edward
2	M	EVANS	Leonard	624		6/25/06								Alias JONES
2	M	EVANS	Robert	193		11/04/1885								
2	M	EVANS	Thomas	340		04/10/1887								
4	F	EWBANK	Clara	C342	51	7/2/03	Scotland		Nurse	Endeavouring to procure charitable contributions by false pretences	14 days HL		CoS	Alias Emily McKAY
4	M	FALLOWS	William	B2	30	4/17/02	Woolwich		Tailor	Stealing jewellery	9 cal months HL		Dissenter	Alias William Albert PRATT
2	M	FARMER	Arthur	2676		25/06/1883								
2	M	FEGAN	James	498		05/04/1895								
4	M	FERRARI	Vincent	C34	32	7/7/03	Italy		Sailor	Stealing two motor car lamps	1 cal month HL		RC	
1	M	FISHER	Walter	148	16	03/05/1870	Churcham	S	Labourer	Maiming a mare	1y Hard Labour	Kingstanley		
4	M	FITZGERALD	John	B978	22	2/14/02	Chatham		Labourer	Stealing a bag & 7 fowls	1 month HL		CoE	Alias BOXALL
2	M	FLETCHER	Thomas	350		08/03/1894								
1	M	FLOYD	Alfred	203	23	06/05/1870	Westbury on Trym	M	Labourer	Stealing cider	1m Hard Labour	Westbury on Trym		
2	M	FLYNN	John Morris	2661		05/01/1884								
4	F	FOLEY	Alice	B934	25	12/29/02	Cardiff		Prostitute	Obtaining money by false pretences	Discharged			
2	M	FOLLOWS	James	16?		13/10/1887								Or FOLLOWS
4	M	FORD	Alfred	C168	24	7/7/03	Plymouth		General smith	Stealing iron boiler, 4 iron window frames, etc.	1 cal month HL		CoE	
2	F	FORMBY	Susannah	22		09/07/1885								Susannah
1	F	FOUNTAIN	Emma	254	24	18/06/1870	Cheltenham	M	None	Obtain Goods by FP	3m Hard Labour	Cheltenham		
2	M	FOX	James											See MALONEY
2	M	FOX	Thomas	416		08/09/1896								
4	M	FRANCIS	Walter	B213	21	5/30/02	Dane Kell?, Sussex		Labourer	Stealing 29lbs of potatoes	1 cal month HL or pay £2 13s		CoE	
4	M	FREDERICKS	Joseph	B182	23	6/20/01	Birmingham		Groom	Stealing a set of harness	21 days HL		CoE	
1	M	FRICKER	Thomas	26	30	30/04/1870	Gloucester	M	Labourer	Stealing barley	1m Hard Labour	Gloucester		
1	M	FRITH	John	20	30	30/04/1870	Eastington	S	Labourer	Stealing watch	20d Hard Labour	Gloucester		
4	M	FROST	Herbert	A137		7/3/1900								
4	M	FRY	Frederick	C72	33	7/7/03	Charfield		Labourer	Stealing clothing	1 cal month HL		CoE	
4	M	FURBER	Thomas	B198	21	6/22/01	Worcester		Painter	Breaking into a chapel with intent to steal	6 weeks HL		Dissenter	Alias John DREDGE
4	M	FURBER	Thomas	B198	21	6/22/01	Worcester		Painter	Breaking into a chapel with intent to steal	6 weeks HL		Dissenter	Alias John DREDGE
2	M	FUREY	Patrick											See Thomas CAFLIN
2	M	GALTON	John	1		11/8/05								

Album	Sex	Surname	Forenames	Ref. No.	Age	Date of Photo	Birthplace	Marital	Occupation	Offence	Sentence	Destination	Religion	Notes
1	M	GARDNER	William	45	22	30/04/1870	Wotton under Edge		Shoemaker	Stealing a watch	1y Hard Labour	Tetbury		
4	M	GARLAND	Francis	B631	48	10/28/01	Bristol		Plasterer	Maliciously damaging a dwelling house	1 Cal month HL		CoE	
2	M	GARRET	William Henry											See William Henry BRADSHAW
2	F	GARRITY	Mary Ann											See LEE
1	M	GIBBS	George	59	18	30/04/1870	Blakeney	S	Collier	Stealing timber	7d Hard Labour	Brearn's Green		
2	M	GILES	Cyprus	565		2/25/02								
2	M	GILL	George Grenadier	407		07/03/1887								Alias Grenadier?
4	M	GILLETT	Albert	B99	21	4/23/02	Down Ampney		Labourer	Burglary	12 months HL		CoE	
4	M	GILLETT	Albert	A962		17/07/1899								
4	M	GILLETT	Albert	A424		4/5/1900								
1	M	GINGELL	Charles Henry	191	9	06/05/1870	Longhope	S	None	Stealing wheat	1m Hard Labour	Longhope		
1	M	GINGELL	Joseph	145	35	03/05/1870	Guiting	M	Gardener	Stealing artichokes	7d Hard Labour	Cheltenham		
2	F	GLOVER	Ann	2710		13/10/1882								
1	M	GOLDING	Joseph	66	60	30/04/1870	Berkeley	M	Labourer	Stealing meat	1m Hard Labour	Berkeley		
2	M	GOODDEN	Matthew	258		16/12/1890	Berkeley		Labourer					
1	M	GOODWIN	Thomas	197	20	06/05/1870	Cheshire	S	Labourer	Stealing meat	2m Hard Labour	Gloucester		
2	M	GOUGH	Alfd. Thos.	442		24/09/1889								
2	M	GOUGH	Alfred	77		20/06/1896								
4	M	GOUGH	Charles	B874	29	8/7/01	Ashleworth		Labourer	Attempting to carnally know an imbecile woman	2 months HL		CoE	
2	M	GOULDING	Stephen											See William CLARKE?
4	M	GRANGER	Richard	1305	39	7/14/04	West Bromwich		Engineer	Felony, forgery	6 months HL	Bristol	Baptist	
1	M	GRANT	James	171	53	03/05/1870	Holcomb Regis	M	Chairmaker	Stealing chair seats	1m Hard Labour	Bristol		
1	M	GRANT	Thomas	210	56	06/05/1870	Canada	S	Labourer	Stealing boots	6w Hard Labour	North Cerney		
1	M	GREEN	Henry	255	30	18/06/1870	Berkshire	M	Gipsy Hawker	Receiving stolen property	3m Hard Labour	Uncertain		Charged with wife Emma – P86
4	M	GREEN	James	C1174	33	4/13/04	Belfast		F. Polisher	Begging	10 days HL		CoE	
2	M	GREEN	William	138	25	29/04/1870	Winchcombe	S	Groom	Stealing a waistcoat	1m Hard Labour	Cirencester		
2	M	GREENWOOD	John	63		10/07/1896								
1	F	GRIFFIN	Ellen	49	18	30/04/1870	Bristol	S	Servant	Stealing ribbon	6w Hard Labour	Cheltenham		
1	F	GRIFFIN	Jane	123	18	29/04/1870	Cheltenham	S	Servant	Stealing Linsey	1m Hard Labour	Cheltenham		
2	M	GRIFFITHS	Edward	306		25/02/1888								
2	M	GRIFFITHS	Edward	378		23/10/1890								
2	M	GRIFFITHS	James	149		15/04/1893								
2	M	GRIFFITHS	Nehemiah	111		11/04/1885								
2	M	GRIFFITHS	Raymond	482		10/22/1900								
2	M	GRISWOOD	Alfred	202		10/19/01								Not in index under G

Album	Sex	Surname	Forenames	Ref. No.	Age	Date of Photo	Birthplace	Marital	Occupation	Offence	Sentence	Destination	Religion	Notes
4	M	GRUNDY	Reginald Joseph	526	20	10/27/04	Hereford		Carpenter	Sheep Stealing	1 month HL		Primitive Methodist	
2	M	GUNDY	William	280	17	03/03/1892	Gloucester	S	Servant	Stealing wearing apparel	3m Hard Labour	Berry Hill, Coleford		
1	F	GWILLIAM	Hannah	159	30	03/05/1870	Beckford		Collier	Forging a request for the delivery of goods	6 months HL		CoE	
4	M	GWYNN	James	C1104	30	7/16/03	London		Printer	Stealing 7s 6d	18 months HL		CoE	
4	M	GWYNN	John	B43	60	8/12/02								
2	M	HADE	John	K66		27/05/1890								
1	M	HAINES	Charles	240	11	04/06/1870	Barnwood	S	None	Stealing money	21d Hard Labour & 12 strikes with birch rod	Barnwood		
Album	Sex	Surname	Forenames	Ref. No.	Age	Date of Photo	Birthplace	Marital	Occupation	Offence	Sentence	Destination	Religion	Notes
2	M	HAINES	Ernest	288	33	29/03/1890	Rodborough	S	Shoemaker	Stealing a locket	6m Hard Labour	Rodborough		
1	M	HAINES	Henry	36	24	30/04/1870	Cheltenham	M	Labourer	Stealing moleskin	1m Hard Labour	Cheltenham		
1	M	HAINES	Thomas	57	24	30/04/1870	Cheltenham	M	Labourer	Stealing a kettle	2m Hard Labour	Cheltenham		
1	M	HAINES	Thomas	202		06/05/1870			Labourer					
2	M	HALL	John	2613		24/03/1883								
1	M	HALL	William E F	102	10	29/04/1870	Australia	S		Stealing a fowl	21d Hard Labour & 5y R	Bourton on Hill		
2	M	HALLAM	John	420		7/30/1900								
2	M	HALSON	Frederick	613		5/5/05								
4	M	HAMILTON	Frank Richard	C573	26	3/29/04	New Zealand		Mental Nurse	Stealing money	6 cal months HL & 3 years police supervision		CoE	
2	M	HANDFORD	Hudson	623		1/5/01								
4	M	HANDS	Alfred	C188	38	12/3/03	Cheshire		Carpenter	Stealing one pair of pliers, one screwdriver, one gold watch	6 cal months HL and 2 years police supervision		CoE	
1	M	HANKWRIGHT	Edward	177	47	03/05/1870	Dudley	M	Collier	Stealing a coat	3m Hard Labour	Stow on the Wold		
2	M	HARPER	Geo.	4152		01/10/1884								
4	M	HARRINGTON	George	B797	21	11/8/02	London		Labourer	Housebreaking and stealing therein 1 piece of soap, 1 pack of cards	12 months HL		CoE	Alias Frank BARBER, George BROWN or GREENAWAY
4	M	HARRINGTON	George	797	21	9/18/03	London		Labourer	Housebreaking and Stealing therein one towel, 1 piece of soap, 1 pack of cards	12 months HL			Alias Frederick BARBER, BROWN, GREENAWAY
2	M	HARRIS	Alfred	2370		29/07/1882							CoE	
4	M	HARRIS	Arthur	B768	28	10/30/02	Leamington		Stoker	Stealing PO bank book, 2 pass books, cheque book and £42	12 cal months HL		CoE	Alias Arthue HARRIS
2	M	HARRIS	Edwin	295		11/03/1898								
	M	HA…	G…	A..8		11/4/1900								

Album	Sex	Surname	Forenames	Ref. No.	Age	Date of Photo	Birthplace	Marital	Occupation	Offence	Sentence	Destination	Religion	Notes
2	M	HARRIS	John	34		12/11/1887								Cond. 16/04/1902 Worksop
2	M	HARRIS	John	387		12/7/1900								18/08/1902 Scarboro' & failed to report/als Brown
2	M	HARRIS	Thomas	139		18/01/1892								
2	M	HARRIS	William	258		28/06/1890								
2	M	HARRIS	William	290		11/8/05								
4	M	HARRIS	William	B474		9/6/01								
2	M	HARRISON	Charles	4423		30/12/1884								
2	F	HARRISON	Jane	11		08/07/1886								
2	M	HARTLAND	John Francis	272		21/04/1894								
2	M	HARVEY	John	260		26/08/1893								
1	M	HATHAWAY	Benjamin	276	19	02/07/1870	London	S	Labourer	Stealing a bank note	6m Hard Labour & 7y Police Supervision	Cheltenham		
4	M	HATTON	Philip	B219	27	8/7/01	Newnham		Mason's labourer	Indecent Assault	2 months HL		CoE	
2	M	HATTON	William	807		22/07/1895								
2	M	HATTON	William	489		30/08/1898								
1	M	HAWKES	Charles	136	19	29/04/1870	Longborough	S	Labourer	Stealing a coat	2m Hard Labour	Longborough		
4	M	HAWKINS	Alfred William	C763	23	3/29/04	London		Woodchopper	Housebreaking	6 cal months HL		CoE	
1	F	HAWKINS	Elizabeth	226	22	14/05/1870	Lydbrook	S	Charwoman	Stealing coal	6m Hard Labour	Lydbrook		
1	F	HAWKINS	Emma	227	17	14/05/1870	Lydbrook	S	Charwoman	Stealing coal	6m Hard Labour	Lydbrook		
1	M	HAYES	Henry	18	30	30/04/1870	Horsley	S	Labourer	Stealing money	1m Hard Labour	Minchinhampton		
4	M	HAYNES	Bela Thomas	C948	24	6/20/03	Bourton on the Water		Brickmaker	Housebreaking & stealing therein one pair of boots	6 cal months HL		CoE	
4	M	HAYNES	Bela Thomas	C513	24	6/14/04	Bourton on the Water		Brickmaker	Housebreaking	9 cal months HL		CoE	
2	M	HAYWARD	Thomas F	414		29/11/1894								
2	M	HEMMINGS	Charles											See William Frederick Doorham
4	M	HENDY	George	C167	39	7/16/03	Kingswood, Bristol		Shoemaker	Warehouse breaking and stealing boots and leather uppers	6 weeks HL		CoE	
1	M	HENDY	John	17	18	30/04/1870	Charfield	S	Labourer	Stealing bread	1m Hard Labour	Charfield		
2	M	HENRY	Charles	524		4/5/06								
2	M	HERBERT	Henry	7		16/09/1886								
4	M	HERBERT	Robert	B512	60	9/2/02	Woolwich		Seaman	Attempted buggery	6 cal months HL		CoE	

Album	Sex	Surname	Forenames	Ref. No.	Age	Date of Photo	Birthplace	Marital	Occupation	Offence	Sentence	Destination	Religion	Notes
2	M	HEWLETT	Frederick											See William Frederick Doorham
2	M	HIGGINBOTTOM	Robert	383		6/12/1900								
2	M	HIGGINBOTTOM	Robert	383		12/7/1900								
4	M	HIGGINS	Thomas	B735	21	10/21/02	Liverpool						RC	
2	M	HIGGINS	William	91		10/12/1896					Stealing one shirt	14 days HL			
2	M	HIGGINS	William Charles	104		21/07/1899									
1	M	HIGGS	John	41	24	30/04/1870	Cheltenham	M	Tailor	Stealing a work box	18m Hard Labour	Cheltenham		
1	M	HILL	Charles	144	14	03/05/1870	Dursley	S	Labourer	Stealing a coat	10d Hard Labour	Dursley		
Album	Sex	Surname	Forenames	Ref. No.	Age	Date of Photo	Birthplace	Marital	Occupation	Offence	Sentence	Destination	Religion	Notes
1	F	HILL	Elizabeth	270	42	02/07/1870	Cheltenham	M	Charwoman	Stealing Bed Linen	6m Hard Labour & 2y Police Supervision	Cheltenham		
1	M	HILL	George	87	14	30/04/1870	Hereford	S	Labourer	Stealing money	1m Hard Labour	Dymock		
1	M	HILL	Thomas	174	18	30/05/1870	Hereford	S	Baker	Embezzlement	1m Hard Labour	Cheltenham		
2	M	HILL	Thomas	R362		24/12/1891									
1	F	HILLIER	Harriet	200	16	05/05/1870	Winterbourne	S	Servant	Stealing a brooch	1m Hard Labour	Newnham		
2	M	HINTON	William	395		01/07/1889									
2	M	HINTON	William	276		22/06/1891									
2	M	HINTON	William	198		13/01/1893									
2	M	HIRONS	William ENoch	322		27/05/1887									
2	M	HODNETT	Edwin	292		01/05/1888									
1	M	HOLBROOK	Thomas	196	19	06/05/1870	Gloucester	S	Hawker	Stealing meat	2m Hard Labour	Gloucester		
1	M	HOLDER	George	218	37	07/05/1870	Chalford	S	Waterman	Stealing gun	2m Hard Labour	Chalford		
1	F	HOLDER	Harriet	43	40	30/04/1870	Yorkshire	M	None	Stealing a bag	1y Hard Labour	Cheltenham		
4	M	HOLDER	Lionel Vivian	B770	19	11/28/02	Gloucester		Clerk	Stealing £7 10s	1 cal month		CoE	
2	M	HOLDER	Samuel	377		22/03/1894									
1	M	HOLLAND	Heartless	108	43	30/04/1870	Warwick	M	Tinker	Stealing hay	7d Hard Labour	Swindon		
2	M	HOLLINSHEAD	Frederick	492		30/08/1898									
2	F	HOLLOWAY	Annie											See Maria Simmons
4	M	HOLLOWAY	J	59		11/14/04	Leckhampton		Gardener	Larceny after PCF	5 months HL			
4	M	HOLLOWAY	John	A311	55	1/1/1900							CoE	
2	M	HOLLOWAY	Thomas	163		12/23/04									
4	M	HOOPER	George	C.1122	23	11/3/03	Moreton in Marsh	M	Labourer	Sheep Stealing	8 cal months HL & 3 years police supervision		CoE	
1	M	HOOPER	Jesse	257	9	18/06/1870	Gloucester	[Blank]	None	Stealing rope	20d & 12 strikes with birch rod	Gloucester		
1	M	HOOPER	Richard	256	46	18/06/1870	Cirencester	S	Labourer	Stealing brass	3m Hard Labour	Cirencester		

Album	Sex	Surname	Forenames	Ref. No.	Age	Date of Photo	Birthplace	Marital	Occupation	Offence	Sentence	Destination	Religion	Notes
2	M	HOPSON	James											See W. Johnson
2	M	HORN	William (James?)	756		11/8/05								
1	M	HOWARD	Henry	211	40	06/05/1870	Manchester	S	Groom	Stealing wrapper	4m Hard Labour	Cheltenham		
1	M	HOWARD	James	114	28	30/04/1870	Liverpool	S	Seaman	Stealing bread	14d Hard Labour	Uncertain		
1	M	HOWELLS	Samuel	167	24	03/05/1870	Worcester	M	Labourer	Stealing meat	9m Hard Labour	Newent		
1	M	HUCKER	James	274	17	02/07/1870	Somerset	S	Labourer	Stealing Ducks	6m Hard Labour & 5y Police Supervision	Bristol		
4	M	HUDD	Isaac	325	23	14/08/1899	Malta		Shoemaker	Stealing 9 fowls; warehouse breaking & stealing 7 pair of boot uppers, etc	12 cal months HL		CoE	
2	M	HUGHES	Thomas											See Alexander Kelly
2	M	HUGHES	Walter	881		7/18/05								
1	M	HULLS	Robert	263	47	25/06/1870	Gloucester	S	Labourer	Receiving	12m Hard Labour	Gloucester		
4	M	HUMPHRIES	William	B721	43	10/29/02	Kingstanley	M	Blacksmith	Stealing 3 fowls	1 cal month HL		CoE	
1	M	HUNTLEY	James	25	47	30/04/1870	Gloucester	S	Labourer	Stealing barley	1m Hard Labour	Gloucester		
1	M	HURCOMBE	Ralph	112	53	30/04/1870	Uley		Labourer	Stealing coal	1m Hard Labour	Uley		
1	M	HURCOMBE	William Henry	40	21	30/04/1870	Gloucester	S	Labourer	Stealing money	18m Hard Labour	Gloucester		
4	M	HYAM	David	B629	17	10/29/02	Gloster		Labourer	Housebreaking and stealing therein 1 gold ring, 1 knife, etc.	6 weeks HL		CoE	
1	F	HYDE	Charlotte	80	20	30/04/1870	Bristol	S	Servant	Housebreaking	1m Hard Labour	Blakeney		
1	M	HYDE	James	5	34	16/04/1870	Cheltenham	M	Labourer	Stealing pigs cheeks	7y Penal Servitude & 7y Police Supervision	[To Pentonville]		
4	M	ILES	William	B1073	27	6/10/02	Cheltenham		Soldier	Stealing two plates, 2 knives, etc.	3 cal months HL		CoE	
1	M	IRELAND	William	192	27	06/05/1870	Chedworth	M	Labourer	Stealing a watch	3m Hard Labour	Chedworth		
4	M	IRELAND	William	EJV37		01/05/1899								
1	M	JACKSON	Francis	205	9	06/05/1870	Upton St Leonards	S	None	Stealing a chicken	10d Hard Labour	Upton St Leonards		
2	M	JACKSON	James	39		28/12/1891								Alias SHAW
1	M	JACKSON	Richard	107	55	30/04/1870	Devon	S	Labourer	Stealing oats and hay	14d Hard Labour	West Dean		
1	M	JAMES	John	264	22	25/06/1870	Lydney	S	Collier	Assault	3m Hard Labour	Forest of Dean		
4	M	JAMESON	George	C686	35	8/6/03	Cardiff		Dealer	Stealing a silver watch from the person	12 cal months HL		CoE	
2	F	JARVIS	Harriet	77	42	27/07/1887	Newcastle on Tyne		Labourer	Stealing overcoat	6 weeks HL			
4	M	JARVIS	Henry	417		7/18/02							CoE	
1	M	JARVIS	James	9	51	30/04/1870	N Wales	M	Nailer	Stealing rabbits	7d Hard Labour	Cirencester		

Album	Sex	Surname	Forenames	Ref. No.	Age	Date of Photo	Birthplace	Marital	Occupation	Offence	Sentence	Destination	Religion	Notes
2	M	JENKINS	Thomas	163		27/08/1888								
2	M	JENKINS	William	375		12/1/05								
2	M	JEYNES	William	73		29/12/1884								
4	M	JOBBINS	Percy	C1012	19	7/16/03	Stratton, WIL		Soldier	Burglariously breaking into a dwelling house and therein stealing one clock	6 months HL		CoE	
4	M	JOEL	Arthur	B784	55	6/10/02	Siddington, GLS		Labourer	Aiding and abetting to steal 3s 9d	6 cal months		CoE	See A Williams
2	M	JOHNS	Samuel	50		11/8/05								
2	M	JOHNS	Thomas											
4	M	JOHNSON	Henry	B489		4/17/02								
2	M	JOHNSON	John	513		9/12/01								Monkey Brand
4	M	JOHNSON	Robert	B531	27	9/2/02	Ireland		Winodw cleaner	Stealing an overcoat, handkerchief, piece of mutton & purse	21 days HL		CoE	
2	M	JOHNSON	William	327		12/1/05								
2	M	JOHNSON	William Henry	91		11/8/05								
2	M	JONES	Albert	406		05/10/1885								
2	M	JONES	Albert	278		28/04/1888								
2	M	JONES	Alfred	640		7/6/06								
2	F	JONES	Annie											
4	M	JONES	Arthur	B785	22	12/31/02	[blank]		Painter	Stealing a coat and vest	2 months HL		CoE	
1	M	JONES	Arthur	275	24	2/07/1870	Littledean	S	Miner	Stealing duck & Fowls	6m Hard Labour & 3y Police Supervision	Forest of Dean		
4	M	JONES	Arthur Henry	B604	18	3/27/02	Bristol		Collier	Stealing a bicycle	6 cal months HL & 1 year Police supervision		CoE	
2	M	JONES	Charles	69		29/06/1885								
2	M	JONES	Charles	188		18/04/1887								
4	F	JONES	Eliza Ann	B489	62	3/27/02	Gloster		Laundress	Stealing one skirt	6 cal months HL		CoE	
2	F	JONES	Elizabeth											
2	M	JONES	George	751		8/23/05								
2	M	JONES	George	627		7/6/06								
2	M	JONES	Henry	246		04/01/1889								
2	M	JONES	Henry											
2	M	JONES	Henry	33		6/19/03								
2	M	JONES	James	331		04/07/1885								
2	M	JONES	James Llewellyn	125		12/08/1891								Also 7.4.79 and 3.88

Album	Sex	Surname	Forenames	Ref. No.	Age	Date of Photo	Birthplace	Marital	Occupation	Offence	Sentence	Destination	Religion	Notes
2	M	JONES	John	2841		26/04/1884								
2	M	JONES	John	62		13/07/1888								Alias PENDRY
2	M	JONES	John	K292		01/02/1889								
2	M	JONES	John	641		7/6/06								
2	M	JONES	Pryce	639		7/6/06								
2	M	JONES	Thomas	3012		30/01/1884								Alias Evans
2	M	JONES	Thomas											
2	M	JONES	Thomas	316		23/05/1890								1891
2	M	JONES	Thomas	234		15/12/1891								
2	M	JONES	Thomas	338		02/12/1893								Or BROWN
2	M	JONES	Thomas	275		13/04/1896								
2	M	JONES	Thomas	4047		7/25/04								
2	M	JONES	Thomas	190		11/8/05								Walter? ASHFORD?
2	M	JONES	William	448		8/10/01								
2	M	JONES	William	696		7/19/06								Transferred from Cardiff 07/09/1906
4	M	JONES	William	A281		2/5/1900								
2	M	JORDAN	John	497		8/24/04								
1	M	JORDAN	Samuel	223	27	07/05/1870	Tewkesbury	S	Labourer	Feloniously Receiving	9m Hard Labour	Gloucester		
1	F	JORDAN	Sarah	99	12	29/04/1870	Cheltenham	S	Servant	Cheat	6w & 5y R	Cheltenham		
2	M	JUBB	William Henry	562		5/24/01								
4	M	KEAR	George	B912	23	5/6/02	Cheltenham		Painter	Forgery	4 months HL		CoE	
2	M	KELLY	Alexander	608		7/4/03								
4	M	KELLY	John	B197	30	5/21/02	London		Labourer	Stealing one ham	21 days HL		CoE	
2	M	KELLY	John	509		01/01/1895								
1	M	KENDALL	Joseph	3	32	16/04/1870	Boddington	M	Labourer	Housebreaking	7y Penal Servitude & 7y Police Supervision	[To Pentonville]		
2	F	KENEDY	Florence	37		29/12/1887								KENNEDY in index. Also DAVIS
2	M	KENT	Frederick William	295		7/30/1900								Just William in index
4	M	KERRIDGE	Arthur	C942	24	11/3/03	Germany		Valet	Burglary and stealing one silver ingot, one wedding ring	12 cal months HL		CoE	
2	M	KEY	Robert	194		11/16/03								

Album	Sex	Surname	Forenames	Ref. No.	Age	Date of Photo	Birthplace	Marital	Occupation	Offence	Sentence	Destination	Religion	Notes
1	M	KIDWELL	Clement	6	45	30/04/1870	Wick & Abson	M	Labourer	Stealing knives	2m Hard Labour	Siston		
1	M	KILMINSTER	Edgar Leopold	268	7	25/06/1870	Chalford	S	None	Stealing Sweetmeats	7d Hard Labour & 12 strikes with birch rod	Chalford		
1	M	KILMINSTER	Joseph William	269	9	25/06/1870	Chalford	S	None	Stealing Sweetmeats	7d Hard Labour & Whipped	Chalford		
4	M	KING	Fonier	B821	28	4/15/02	Canada		Civil engineer	Obtaining wearing apparel by false pretences	4 cal months HL		CoE	
2	M	KING	Fonier	409		8/17/03								
2	M	KING	George	641		14/04/1896								
1	M	KINGDOM	James	63	25	30/04/1870	Plymouth	M	Gardener	Stealing a hoe	3m Hard Labour	Horfield		
4	M	KINSEY	Daniel Henry	C1183	77	2/3/04	Leminster		Builder	Stealing one silver paten? And one silver box	12 cal months HL and 5 years police supervision		Congregationalist	
	M	KINSMAN	John											Or Harris
2	M	KIRK	George	B818	25	8/4/02	London		Electrician	Shopbreaking & stealing shirts	8 cal months HL		CoE	
4	M	KNIGHT	Francis	B365	32	8/13/01	London		Labourer	Stealing bacon value 1/-	2 months HL		CoE	KNIGHT in nominal register
1	M	KNIGHT	William	248	20	11/06/1870	London	S	Labourer	Stealing 9d from master	1m Hard Labour	Wolastone		
2	M	LAKIN	Frederick John	197		10/28/03								
4	F	LANCASTER	Ellen	4190		27/06/1884								
4	M	LANCASTER	George	B719	37	4/25/02	Greverall, WIL		Shepherd	Attempted murder and suicide	6 months; 3rd division		CoE	
2	M	LANDER	George William	193		10/28/03								
2	M	LANE	Frederick	329		23/01/1891								
2	M	LANE	Frederick	113		17/10/1893								
4	M	LANE	John	B464	45	10/21/01	Ashleworth		Labourer	Stealing 3 fowls	1 cal month HL		CoE	
1	F	LANE	Maria	232	17	21/05/1870	Gloucester	S	Servant	Stealing gloves & other items	1m Hard Labour	Gloucester		
1	M	LANG	Charles	97	36	28/04/1870	Germany	S	Hawker	Stealing pictures	6m Hard Labour	London		
4	M	LASBURY	Sidney Alf	351	17	7/25/04	Stroud		Presser	Stealing money, 24s after PCF	2 months HL		CoE	
1	M	LAW	Robert	55	16	30/04/1870	Fairford	S	Labourer	Stealing gin	1m Hard Labour	Fairford		
2	M	LAWSON	George	480		25/11/1898								
2	M	LEA	Thomas	222		12/06/1890								

Album	Sex	Surname	Forenames	Ref. No.	Age	Date of Photo	Birthplace	Marital	Occupation	Offence	Sentence	Destination	Religion	Notes
1	M	LEDIARD	Herod	245		25/06/1870								Alias GARRITY
2	F	LEE	Mary A.	2707		05/07/1883								Alias Buster
2	M	LEE	William	626		23/03/1899								Alias Buster
2	M	LEE	William	74		12/14/01								q/195
2	M	LEONARD	William	Q195		19/07/1890								
2	M	LEWIS	Alfred Weyman	680		5/21/03								
4	M	LEWIS	Charles Henry	A168		10/07/1899								
4	M	LEWIS	John Spare	B362	43	8/12/02	Liverpool		Bank Manager	Embezzling £500, £130, £100	12 cal months HL		CoE	Alias Frederick BARBER?
2	M	LEWIS	Richard											Or SAGE or SMITH
2	M	LEWIS	Samuel	235		7/16/06								Transferred from Cardiff 07/09/1906. Cardiff Reg. No. 235
2	M	LEWIS	Thomas	36		08/02/1886								
2	M	LEWIS	Thomas	610		3/3/03								
2	M	LEWIS	William	2763		26/04/1883								
2	M	LIMBRICK	Albert Edward	353		9/22/04								
4	M	LITTLEY	Thomas	537	20	8/19/04	London		Carman	Stealing money, 15/10	3 months HL		CoE	
4	M	LIVINGSTONE	John Henry William	C267	16	9/9/03	Plymouth		Tailor	Stealing one sack, 24 glass bottles and 130lbs of rags	3 cal months HL		RC	
2	M	LLOYD	Edward	Q196		19/07/1890								q/196
2	M	LLOYD	George	238		03/07/1893								
2	M	LLOYD	George Richard											See EVANS
1	M	LLOYD	William	30	52	30/04/1870	Mitcheldean	M	Carpenter	Stealing timber	14d Hard Labour	East Dean		
1	M	LODGE	Charles	61	27	30/04/1870	Tibberton	S	Labourer	Stealing cider	7d Hard Labour	Tibberton		
4	M	LONG	Robert	A58	18	09/08/1899	Berkeley	S	Labourer	Cheat – obtain goods on FP	6m Hard Labour	Berkeley		
1	M	LONGSTREET	William	272		02/07/1870								
1	M	LORD	William	251	80	11/06/1870	Berks	S	Labourer	Stealing timber	6m Hard Labour (&7y Police Supervision)	Kempstead (sic)		HM Free pardon on grounds of ill health
4	M	LOUD	Elijah	352	23	9/22/04	Not known		Porter	Embezzlement	4 months HL		Congregationalist	Or LOUIL?
2	M	LOVELL	Joshua	773		11/8/05								
1	M	LOVESY	James	31	13	30/04/1870	Prestbury	S	Errand Boy	Stealing tobacco	10d Hard Labour	Cheltenham		

Album	Sex	Surname	Forenames	Ref. No.	Age	Date of Photo	Birthplace	Marital	Occupation	Offence	Sentence	Destination	Religion	Notes
1	M	LOW	Charles	118	13	30/04/1870	London		None	Stealing sweets	10d Imprisonment & R	Kingswood		
2	M	LOWRIE	Frederick	208	26	12/14/01	Dorhead, WIL		Farm labourer	Rogue & vagabond; exposing his person	6 weeks HL		CoE	
4	M	LUCAS	Thomas	B1246	47	5/5/02	Bisley		Dealer	Forging an endorsement on an order for £41	2 months HL		CoE	
4	M	LUGG	James Michael Arthur	B876		3/18/02								
1	M	LUSTY	Edward	11	24	30/04/1870	Kingstanley	M	Labourer	Stealing bread	7d Hard Labour	Kingstanley		Alias Edward Knee
4	M	MACKAY	Alexander	B491	48	8/22/02	Scotland		Labourer	Stealing one thatching knife	14 days HL		CoE	Alias John BROWN
2	M	MACKENZIE	Robert	607		3/20/03								
2	M	MACKLIN	John	177		19/08/1897								
1	M	MADDEN	Jeremiah	279	50	02/07/1870	Ireland	S	Labourer	Stealing Iron	2m Hard Labour	Coleford		
2	M	MAGUIRE	Hugh John	182		21/09/1899								Or McGUIRE
2	M	MALONEY	James Thomas	301		21/04/1887								Alias MALONEY!
2	M	MANSELL	John	249		23/07/1888								
2	M	MAPP	John	126		16/04/1889								
4	M	MAPPS	George J	XDNU		1899								
1	M	MARINI	Andrew	184	24	03/05/1870	Italy	S	Seaman	Maliciously wounding	14d Hard Labour	Uncertain		
4	M	MARLOW	John	B579	43	10/28/01	Bristol		Labourer	Stealing clock weights	1 Cal month HL		CoE	
4	M	MARSH	Joseph	C266	25	10/9/03	St Helens, lancs		Labourer	Stealing one sack, 24 glass bottles and 130lbs of rags	4 cal months HL		RC	
1	M	MARSHALL	Charles	58	13	30/04/1870	Cheltenham	S	Labourer	Stealing books	10d Hard Labour & whipped	Gloucester		
2	M	MARSTON	Samuel	137		1/23/03								
4	M	MARTIN	Charles	A161		10/3/1900								
1	M	MARTIN	Daniel	46	37	30/04/1870	Cheltenham		Plasterer	Stealing money	1y Hard Labour	Cheltenham		
2	F	MARTIN	Margaret	74		01/07/1895								
4	M	MARTIN	Thomas	B229	29	5/27/02	Birmingham	M	Labourer	Stealing a dog	3 months HL		CoE	Alias HARRINGTON
4	M	MASON	Alfred	140		8/19/04								
2	F	MASON	Martha	81		15/04/1886								
2	F	MASON	Martha	NQ4		04/11/1890								
4	M	MASON	William	A1015		15/06/1899								
4	M	MASTERS	Charles	734	27	10/4/04	London		Porter	Stealing money, about £1.15s	1 month HL		CoE	

Album	Sex	Surname	Forenames	Ref. No.	Age	Date of Photo	Birthplace	Marital	Occupation	Offence	Sentence	Destination	Religion	Notes
4	M	MATTHEWS	John	B201	24	5/21/02	Salisbury		Labourer	Stealing one ham, assaulting one Harry Moss	21 days HL		CoE	
4	M	MATTHEWS	John	993	27	7/21/02	Ireland		Labourer	Stealing 2 dozen glass tumblers, 3 gas brackets, 10 door keys	6 months HL		RC	Alias Michael FEINEY, Thomas ARNETT
1	F	MAY	Mary	103	45	30/04/1870	Ireland	M	None	Stealing a coat	6w Hard Labour	Cheltenham		
1	F	MAY	Mary	166	45	3/05/1870	Ireland	M	None	Stealing a dress	21d Hard Labour	Cheltenham		
4	M	McDONALD	Henry	C1341	24	6/14/04	Glasgow		Stoker	Stealing china tea service and tools	3 months HL		CoE	Alias Ernest HOLTON
2	F	McKENNA	Catharine	39		29/09/1888								
2	M	McKENZIE	Robert											See R RILEY
2	M	McKINDER	William Henry											See BRADSHAW & GARRET / Or LANE
2	M	McLEAN	James	154?		28/10/1887								
2	M	McLEAN	James	39		11/16/03								
2	M	McSHEEDY	Austin	44		30/10/1899								
4	M	MEDLICOTT	Frederick	A235		13/10/1899								
2	M	MEMORY	Stephen	1048		24/09/1897								
2	M	MERCHANT	Daniel	223		10/28/03								
1	M	MERCHANT	Henry	69	17	30/04/1870	Cirencester	S	Tramp	Stealing money	3m Hard Labour	Uncertain		
4	M	MERIDITH	Charles	B1244	29	3/29/02	London		Electrical engineer	Obtaining board and lodging by false pretences	4 cal months HL		CoE	Alias Charles PREEST, George FITZGERALD, Thomas SCHICK
2	M	MERRIDAY	John											See George COOPER
1	F	MERRIMAN	Elizabeth	115	36	30/04/1870	Cheltenham	S	Pauper	Stealing soap	14d Hard Labour	Cheltenham		
1	M	MERRITT	Samuel George	4	22	16/04/1870	Stroud	S	Clothworker	Stealing boots	7y Penal Servitude & 7y Police Supervision	[To Pentonville]		
2	M	MILES	William											See EVANS, BROWN, MILES, MORGAN, JONES!
1	F	MILLARD	Eliza	125	25	29/04/1870	Stapleton	S	Charwoman	Stealing handkerchiefs	1m Hard Labour	Bristol		
2	M	MILLER	Archibald	665		14/12/1895								
4	M	MILLINER	Alfred Ernest	1242	29	7/14/04	Tockington		Bricklayer	Felony – Larceny in dwelling house	6 months HL		CoE	

Album	Sex	Surname	Forenames	Ref. No.	Age	Date of Photo	Birthplace	Marital	Occupation	Offence	Sentence	Destination	Religion	Notes
1	M	MILLINGTON	John	24	30	30/04/1870	Bangor, Wales	S	Chemist	Stealing forks	6w Hard Labour	Uncertain (a Tramp)		
1	M	MILLS	Charles	273	17	02/07/1870	Bristol	S	Shoemaker	Stealing Ducks	6m Hard Labour & 5y Police Supervision	Bristol		
1	M	MILLS	Charles	7	27	30/04/1870	Stroud	M	Collier	Stealing geese	1m Hard Labour	Cinderford		
2	M	MILLS	William	39		11/8/05								
2	M	MILLWOOD	Henry											See EVANS, BROWN, MILES, MORGAN, JONES!
2	M	MILTON	Edward	454		1/27/06								
4	F	MILTON	Elizabeth	B110	38	7/10/01	Cardiff		Charing	Stealing 3 pairs of trousers	1 month HL		CoE	
2	M	MINTON	William	310		02/07/1888								
1	M	MITCHELL	Alfred	121	26	29/04/1870	Painswick	M	Stonemason	Stealing fowls	2m Hard Labour	Painswick		
4	M	MITCHELL	Samuel	C773	26	11/3/03	[blank]		Labourer	Stealing vest	1 cal month HL		CoE	
4	M	MITCHELL	Walter	B595	17	1/1/03	Cheltenham		Labourer	Breaking into a schoolhouse and stealing therein 9s 6d	3 cal months HL		CoE	
1	M	MITCHELL	William	60	19	30/04/1870	Tibberton	S	Labourer	Stealing cider	7d Hard Labour	Tibberton		
2	M	MITCHELL	William	391	20	20/06/1896	Cheltenham							
1	F	MOLE	Emily	19		30/04/1870	Cheltenham	S	Servant	Stealing money	1m Hard Labour	Cheltenham		
2	M	MOLE	William											See SHINN
4	M	MONA	Frederick R	540	40	8/19/04	Hackney		Painter	Stealing two pairs of boots	1 month HL		CoE	
4	M	MONTAGUE	Leonard	C1342	26	6/14/04	London		Porter	Stealing china tea service and tools	3 months HL		CoE	
4	M	MOORE	Andrew	B338	54	8/19/01	Wrexham		Pedlar	Attempted carnal knowledge of a girl	12 months HL		CoE	
1	M	MOREFIELD	John	216	26	07/05/1870	Sandhurst	M	Labourer	Stealing potatoes	20d Hard Labour	Hull		
1	M	MORGAN	Alfred	2	39	19/04/1870	Cheltenham	M	Painter	Stealing 9 knives	6m Hard Labour & 1y Penal Servitude	Cheltenham		
1	M	MORGAN	Charles	53	11	30/04/1870	Milford	S	Stable boy	Stealing a watch	1m Hard Labour & whipped	Cleve		
4	M	MORGAN	Edward	824	27	9/19/04	Birmingham		Iron worker	Obtaining food by false pretences	12 months HL		Wesleyan	

Album	Sex	Surname	Forenames	Ref. No.	Age	Date of Photo	Birthplace	Marital	Occupation	Offence	Sentence	Destination	Religion	Notes
2	M	MORGAN	Godfrey	AIP1255		13/08/1889								See EVANS, BROWN, MILES, MORGAN, JONES!
4	M	MORGAN	James	C992	20	1/12/03	Hoxton, London		Joiner	Stealing a silver watch from the person	5 years Penal Servitude		CoE	Charles FENLEY alias James MORGAN
4	M	MORGAN	John	B193	19	9/6/01	Lydbrook		Collier	Housebreaking	3 months HL		CoE	
2	M	MORGAN	John	301		2/25/02								
2	M	MORGAN	Oliver	300		4/25/02								
1	F	MORGAN	Sarah	143	12	03/05/1870	Wallingford	S	Tramp	Stealing shirts	10d Hard Labour	Uncertain		
2	M	MORRIS	Charles	540		08/09/1896								
2	M	MORRIS	Charles	326		20/06/1898								
4	M	MORRIS	George	767	18	15/06/1899	London		Labourer	Breaking into a counting house and stealing lead piping	6 cal months HL		CoE	Alias George Anthony COX
Album	Sex	Surname	Forenames	Ref. No.	Age	Date of Photo	Birthplace	Marital	Occupation	Offence	Sentence	Destination	Religion	Notes
2	M	MORRIS	Henry	2677		25/06/1883								Alias WARNER
2	M	MORRIS	Henry	40		28/12/1891								Alias COOK Percy
2	M	MORRIS	Thomas	2953		11/07/1883								
2	M	MORRIS	Thos.	4550		17/04/1885								
2	M	MORRIS	Walter											See Samuel SMITH
4	M	MORRISH	John Bartlett	1144	16	7/21/02	Little Weston?, Somerset		Farmer's assistant	Stealing £12	4 cal months HL		CoE	
1	M	MOSEN	Oliver	176	18	03/05/1870	Bourton on the Water	S	Labourer	Stealing ducks	3m Hard Labour	Bourton on the Water		
1	F	MOSS	Mary Ann	124	15	29/04/1870	Clayhill	S	Char-girl	Stealing handkerchiefs	1m Hard Labour	Stapleton		
1	F	MOTT	Ann	126	19	29/04/1870	Cheltenham	S	Charwoman	Stealing a pair of boots	14d Hard Labour	Cheltenham		
1	F	MOTT	Catherine Ann	237	17	04/06/1870	Cheltenham	S	Charwoman	Stealing meat	2m Hard Labour	Cheltenham		
4	M	MOYNIHAN	James	A544		11/2/1900								
4	M	MOYNIHAN	James	A544		4/30/01								
4	M	MURPHY	Thomas	B575	20	10/5/01	Cork		Labourer	Stealing a coat	1 Cal month HL		RC	
2	M	MURPHY	Thomas											See Richard BIRD
2	M	MYTTON	Albert	461		3/5/06								
4	M	NASH	George	B777	30	3/12/02	Cheltenham		Labourer	Indecent assault	3 cal months HL		CoE	Alias HARPER
2	M	NASH	Thomas	2809		30/06/1883								

Album	Sex	Surname	Forenames	Ref. No.	Age	Date of Photo	Birthplace	Marital	Occupation	Offence	Sentence	Destination	Religion	Notes
1	F	NELMES	Mary Ann	158	16	03/05/1870	Coleford			Stealing coal	7d Hard Labour	Coleford		
2	M	NELSON	Harry	410		1/8/06								
4	M	NEWMAN	Jacob	B1112	36	6/23/02	Mangotsfield		Labourer	Stealing one finger ring, one purse and 7s 9d	3 cal months HL		CoE	
2	M	NICHOLAS	William	393		12/4/05								
4	M	NICHOLLS	Frederick W	A611		3/5/1900								
4	M	NICHOLLS	Frederick William	B751	25	6/10/02	Brockworth, Glos		Baker	Stealing a waterproof coat	8 months HL		CoE	
2	M	NOBLE	William	209		10/19/01								Not in Index
1	F	NORTON	Jane	207	27	06/05/1870	Lechlade	M	Washer	Stealing table cloth	3m Hard Labour	Gloucester		
4	M	NUTBURN	Mark	B977	28	2/14/02	Southampton		Labourer	Stealing a bag & 7 fowls	1 month HL		CoE	
1	M	O'BRIEN	David	220	17	07/05/1870	Bucks	S	Labourer	Stealing rabbit skins	3m Hard Labour	Stroud		
4	F	OGDEN	Ellen	A227		18/09/1899								
4	M	O'HAGAN	David	A471		1/1/1900								
4	M	O'HAGAN	David	A530		4/30/01	Cheltenham or Cardiff?						RC or CoE?	See 1903; absconding from workhouse; sleeping out
4	F	OLAND	Mary Jane	B1061	30	1/20/03	Kempsford		Needlewoman	Burglary	12 months HL		CoE	
1	M	O'LEARY	Cornelius	130	29	29/04/1870	Ireland	M	Labourer	Stealing coal	6w Hard Labour	Lydney		Transferred from Ipswich prison
2	M	OLIVER	James	451		01/06/1888								
1	M	OLSEN	Sevan	10	23	30/04/1870	Norway	S	Seaman	Stealing a bag	5d Hard Labour	Uncertain		
4	M	O'MORE	Roger	229	34	14/08/1899	Dursley		Coach painter	Burglary	15 cal months HL		CoE	
2	M	O'NEILL	Michael	13		8/28/01								Or O'NIELL
2	M	O'NEILL	Michael	131		9/2/02								
2	M	O'NIEL	John											See George COOPER
1	M	ORGAN	John	250	26	11/06/1870	Badgeworth	M	Labourer	Stealing nails	14d Hard Labour	Badgeworth		
2	M	ORPWOOD	James											See C HENRY
1	F	O'RYAN	Mary	222	36	07/05/1870	Southsea	M	Tramp	Cheat	1m Hard Labour	Brompton		
2	M		Francis	203		10/26/03								
4	M	OSBORNE	James	C306	36	8/6/03	Kingswood, Glos		Shoemaker	Stealing one hammer, one line brush, etc.	2 cal months HL		CoE	
2	M	OSBORNE	James	297	38	8/19/04	Kingswood		Shoemaker	Stealing Lead after PCF	3 months HL		CoE	
2	M	OSBORNE	John	J44		17/03/1893								
1	M	OTTON	George	100	26	29/04/1870	Cheltenham	M	Labourer	Stealing ferrets	6w Hard Labour	Cheltenham		

Album	Sex	Surname	Forenames	Ref. No.	Age	Date of Photo	Birthplace	Marital	Occupation	Offence	Sentence	Destination	Religion	Notes
2	M	OWEN	Benjamin											See MANSELL
2	M	OWEN	Frederick William John	233		16/07/1888								Or OWENS
2	M	PAGE	Harry	324	20	7/5/02	Cirencester	S	Labourer	Stealing bags	1m Hard Labour	Cirencester		
1	M	PAISH	Charles	139	21	29/04/1870	Cirencester	S	Basket Maker	Housebreaking and stealing	12m Hard Labour	Tetbury		Apprehended Chedworth
1	M	PAISH	Henry Matthew	261		25/06/1870	Berkeley		Boatman	Lodging in an Outhouse	3 months HL		CoE	
4	M	PALMER	William	786	71	11/14/04	Berkeley		Boatman	Stealing one flask basket, one hammer	2 months HL		CoE	
4	M	PALMER	William	C896	72	1/4/04								
1	M	PARKINSON	George	246	24	11/06/1870	Liverpool	S	Cab Driver	Stealing wearing apparel	2m & 4w Hard Labour	Leamington, WAR		
2	M	PARR	Christopher	81		4/25/02								Photo missing
2	M	PARRY	Samuel											
2	M	PARSONS	James	242		28/07/1885								
2	M	PARSONS	Stephen	243		02/03/1891								
1	F	PARTRIDGE	Ann	137	35	29/04/1870	Gloucester	S	Housekeeper	Stealing money	2m Hard Labour	Gloucester		
1	M	PARTRIDGE	Walter	119	15	30/04/1870	Kingswood	S	Labourer	Stealing money	10d Imprisonment	Kingswood		
2	M	PASSEY	George	35		9/4/03								
1	M	PATES	Thomas	233	44	21/05/1870	Cheltenham	M	Gardener	Stealing scythe & billhook	1m Hard Labour	Cheltenham		
1	M	PAYNE	James	110	40	30/04/1870	Westbury on Trym	M	Sawyer	Stealing tools	4m Hard Labour	Westbury on Trym		
2	F	PAYNE	Mary Ann	2709		29/06/1883								
4	M	PAYTON	Albert	B1107	18	5/5/02	Cheltenham		Labourer	Shopbreaking and stealing therein £1 12s 1d	6 weeks HL		CoE	Alias JARVIS, FREEMAN
4	M	PEARCE	George	A258		10/07/1899								
4	M	PEARCE	John	A564		01/11/1899								
4	M	PELLING	John	732	19	10/15/03	Woolwich		Labourer	Stealing sheet lead	6 weeks HL		CoE	
4	M	PENNINGTON	Alfred	560		11/12/04								
2	M	PENRY	John	K292		01/02/1889								Or PENDRY. Alias JONES
2	M	PERKS	Ernest	275		5/31/02								
1	M	PHELPS	Manfred	160	30	03/05/1870	Gloucester	S	Labourer	Stealing wearing apparel	5m Hard Labour	Gloucester		Once a soldier in the Guards
4	M	PHILLIPS	Francis John	B585	24	10/4/01	Herefordshire		Fitter	Stealing a bicycle	9 cal months HL		Dissenter	
4	M	PHILLIPS	Francis John	B585	24	6/10/02	Herefordshire		Fitter	Stealing a bicycle	9 cal months HL		Dissenter	

Album	Sex	Surname	Forenames	Ref. No.	Age	Date of Photo	Birthplace	Marital	Occupation	Offence	Sentence	Destination	Religion	Notes
1	M	PHILLIPS	James	154	14	03/05/1870	Bristol	S	Labourer	Embezzlement	1m & R	Bristol		
2	M	PHILLIPS	Thomas	577		6/7/02	Newent		grocer's assistant	Embezzling £1	6 weeks HL		CoE	
4	M	PHILLIPS	William	B261	30	11/7/01								
2	M	PHILLIPS	William	563		11/14/01								
2	M	PHILLIPS	William	645		5/1/03								
2	M	PIEPHO	Bernhard	144		14/10/1889								
1	F	PINCHIN	Sarah	84	19	30/04/1870	Cheltenham	S	Servant	Stealing wearing apparel	12w Hard Labour	Cheltenham		
4	M	PITCHER	Arthur	A435		9/25/1900								
4	F	POCKET	Florence	B93	30	7/10/01	Manchester		None	Stealing a child's mail cart	6 weeks HL		CoE	
4	F	POCKETT	Florence	C1050	32	3/23/04	Manchester		None	Larceny after a P C F	3 cal months HL		CoE	
1	M	POLLARD	James	161	17	03/05/1870	Gloucester	S	Nailer	Stealing a tobacco box	14d Hard Labour	Gloucester		
4	M	POOL	William	353	37	7/25/04	Kingswood		Shoemaker	Stealing Lead after PCF	2 months HL		CoE	
2	M	POOLE	Arthur	430		10/22/1900								Alias BURRINGTON
4	M	POPE	Alfred	B33	36	4/17/02	Liverpool		Plasterer	Stealing one 2ft rule, 1 ink bottle, etc	21 days HL		CoE	Alias Hy Atkins, Walter or Thomas Jones, Henry Taylor
4	M	PORTER	Ivo Vane	366	23	9/22/04	Aldsworth		Postman	Larceny whilst employed under Post Office	4 months HL			
4	M	PORTER	Robert	B578	41	10/28/01	Bristol		Labourer	Stealing clock weights	1 Cal month HL		CoE	
2	M	POWELL	David	100		20/06/1898								
2	M	POWELL	George	346		21/07/1886								Alias David CASTREE
1	M	POWELL	Thomas	189	33	06/05/1870	Ross	M	Groom	Stealing oats	6m Hard Labour	Kingswood nr Bristol	CoE	
2	M	POWELL	Thomas Joseph	89		11/07/1888								
1	M	PREADY	Henry	8	25	30/04/1870	Coleford	M	Collier	Stealing geese	1m Hard Labour	Ruardean		
2	M	PREECE	Alfred	524		05/11/1894								
2	M	PREEDY	Charles	S72		29/03/1892								
2	M	PRESBURY	Albert	19		10/13/03								Joining From Worcester
2	M	PRICE	Charles	400		12/7/1900								
2	M	PRICE	Francis	4489		05/02/1885								
2	M	PRICE	Frank	38		08/01/1887								Not in Index
2	M	PRICE	John	U226		11/16/03								

Album	Sex	Surname	Forenames	Ref. No.	Age	Date of Photo	Birthplace	Marital	Occupation	Offence	Sentence	Destination	Religion	Notes
4	M	PRICE	John	A5		18/09/1899								
4	M	PRICE	John	A641		11/1/1900								
4	M	PRICE	John	A641		11/1/1900								
2	F	PRICE	Susan	115		23/03/1895								
1	M	PRICE	William	252	18	18/06/1870	London	S	Clerk	Burglary	6m Hard Labour	Cheltenham		
2	M	PRINCE	William	532		11/7/02								
2	M	PRITCHARD	John Coleman	43		7/28/03								Re-arrested at Bodmin & again at hereford for Bristol Col.
2	F	PRITCHARD	Theresa	37		28/01/1886								
1	M	PRITCHARD	William	74	40	30/04/1870	Monmouth	S	Hawker	Stealing shovels	2m Hard Labour	Uncertain (tramp)		
2	M	PROBERT	Charles Henry											See William MINTON
2	M	PROSSER	William	264		29/02/1888								
Album	Sex	Surname	Forenames	Ref. No.	Age	Date of Photo	Birthplace	Marital	Occupation	Offence	Sentence	Destination	Religion	Notes
4	F	PUFFETT	Alice	B265	23	11/7/01	Filkins, OXF		Servant	Obtaining wearing apparel by false pretences	6 weeks HL		CoE	
4	M	PURNELL	Henry	B29	32	9/29/02	Bristol		Collier	Stealing 3 ropes, 124 lbs of iron bolts, 71 lbs of nails	6 cal months HL		CoE	
1	M	PYSER	George	96	29	28/04/1870	Poland	M	Cap Maker	Stealing pictures	6m Hard Labour	Liverpool		
2	M	QUAINTON	Herbert E	411		1/8/06								
4	M	RADFORD	Harry	B1216	60	3/21/02	Bristol		Oil refiner	Stealing one pair of boots	2 months HL		CoE	
2	M	RADFORD	Harry											Alias Joseph Radford? See Richard Bird
1	M	RAYNER	George	44	43	30/04/1870	Cheltenham	S	Groom	Stealing money	12m Hard Labour	Cheltenham		
2	M	REA	George	2929		30/06/1884								
2	M	READ	James	357		25/02/1888								
1	F	REEKS	Ellen	131	14	29/04/1870	Woolastone	S	Servant	Stealing money	1m Hard Labour	Lydney		
1	F	REES	Ann	90	45	28/04/1870	Stourport	M	None	Stealing spoons	3m Hard Labour	Gloucester		
1	M	REEVES	James	238	44	04/06/1870	Blockley	M	Labourer	Stealing barley	2m Hard Labour	Blockley		
2	M	REIDY	John	32		6/19/03								
2	F	RIDLEY	Emily	22		21/04/1890								
2	M	RILEY	Robert	151		11/8/05								

Album	Sex	Surname	Forenames	Ref. No.	Age	Date of Photo	Birthplace	Marital	Occupation	Offence	Sentence	Destination	Religion	Notes
1	M	ROACH	James	51	30	30/04/1870	Cheltenham	M	Painter	Stealing carriage lining	2m Hard Labour	Cheltenham		
1	M	ROBBINS	John	164	39	03/05/1870	Lydney	S	Seaman	Stealing a waistcoat	10d Hard Labour	Uncertain		
1	F	ROBERTS	Mary Ann	78	15	30/04/1870	Cheltenham	S	Char-girl	Stealing a blanket	14d Hard Labour	Cheltenham		
1	F	ROBERTS	Rosina	183	16	03/05/1870	Broadway	S	Servant	Stealing currants	10d Hard Labour	Campden		Not in Index
2	F	ROBERTS	Sarah Ann	71		3/17/05								
2	M	ROBERTS	William	166		11/09/1899								
2	M	ROBERTS	William	166		12/7/1900								
2	M	ROBINSON	John	36		02/04/1891								
4	M	ROGERS	Christopher	A412		11/1/1900								
4	M	ROSE	Henry	B17	50	9/6/01	Bristol		Labourer	Robbery with Violence	3 months HL		CoE	
2	M	ROSS	James	442		16/05/1899								
2	M	ROSSER	Henry	480		3/5/06								
2	M	ROWE	Samuel	P496		16/12/1889								
Album	Sex	Surname	Forenames	Ref. No.	Age	Date of Photo	Birthplace	Marital	Occupation	Offence	Sentence	Destination	Religion	Notes
4	M	ROWLAND	James	222	30	7/25/04	London		Labourer	Breaking into a stable and stealing a pair of clippers	2 months HL		CoE	
	M	RUDGE	Sidney											See Smith
1	M	RUMMINS	George	23	16	30/04/1870	Iron Acton	S	Labourer	Stealing a whip	1m Hard Labour	Yate		
2	M	RUTTER	Thomas											See Thomas Lee
2	F	RYAN	Susan	29		27/10/1888								
2	M	RYAN	Thomas											See thomas Jenkins
2	M	SADLER	William	591		1/23/03								
2	M	SAGE	Henry											See Thomas SMITH
4	M	SAMPSON	James	B20	40	7/10/01	Milton on Thames, Kent		Commercial traveller	Obtaining 10s by false pretences	1 Cal month HL		CoE	
4	M	SAMPSON	James Balster Udal	C1149	43	4/30/04	Kent		Commission Agent	Undischarged bankrupt obtaining credit without disclosing the fact	4 months HL		CoE	
2	M	SANDALL	William I? L	318		25/11/1898								
4	M	SANDERS	John	B483	37	8/18/02	Cheltenham		Labourer	Stealing one hair clipping machine	14 days 3rd Div. Or pay £1.8s		CoE	
1	M	SARGEANT	William	47	23	30/04/1870	Cheltenham	S	Tailor	Housebreaking	1y Hard Labour	Cheltenham		
4	M	SARONEY	Frederick	C1501	18	5/13/04	Cheltenham		Labourer	House breaking	2 months HL	Cheltenham	CoE	
1	M	SAUNDERS	Charles	70	33	30/04/1870	Stroud	M	Labourer	Stealing lead	2m Hard Labour	Cheltenham		
2	M	SAUNDERS	John	P497		16/12/1887								

Sex	Surname	Forenames	Ref. No.	Age	Date of Photo	Birthplace	Marital	Occupation	Offence	Sentence	Destination	Religion	Notes	Album
M	SCHMID	Edward	B1237	32	3/29/02	Switzerland		Dentist	Obtaining board and lodging by false pretences	1 month HL		CoE		4
M	SCOTT	Albert	296	34	11/29/04	Bath		Labourer	Housebreaking and stealing therein after PCF	6 months HL		CoE		4
M	SCOTT	John	C1343	31	4/13/04	Richmond		Labourer	Stealing china tea service and tools	1 month HL		CoE		4
M	SCOTT	William	128	27	29/04/1870	Almondsbury	S	Labourer	Stealing coal	7d Imprisonment	Patchway			1
M	SCRIVEN	Jabez Thomas	37	17	30/04/1870	Eldersfield	S	Labourer	Stealing a cheese	6m Hard Labour	Tibberton			1
M	SEARLE	William	847	23	3/19/04	Epsom		Jockey	Burglariously breaking into a dwelling house and therein stealing money & stamps	18 cal months HL		CoE		4
M	SELBY	George	A754		7/25/1900									4
F	SELLICK	Susan	77	26	30/04/1870	Bridgewater	S	Servant	Stealing a shawl	2m Hard Labour	Cheltenham			1
Sex	Surname	Forenames	Ref. No.	Age	Date of Photo	Birthplace	Marital	Occupation	Offence	Sentence	Destination	Religion	Notes	Album
F	SHEARMAN	Eliza	22	18	30/04/1870	Stroud	S	Needlewoman	Stealing wearing apparel	1m Hard Labour	Stroud			1
F	SHELLARD	Jane	39	54	30/04/1870	Plymouth	W	Laundress	Stealing bedding	18m Hard Labour	Cheltenham			1
M	SHEPPARD	Thomas	52	29	30/04/1870	Bristol	M	Painter	Stealing paint	1m Hard Labour	Bristol			1
M	SHERRINGTON	Henry P?	1051		24/09/1897									2
F	SHIELD	Mary	234	21	21/05/1870	Birmingham	M	Tramp	Stealing a slop?	14d Hard Labour	Cheltenham			1
M	SHIELS	Moses	669		13/04/1895									2
M	SHINN	William	21		29/06/1891								Vide MOLE	2
M	SHIPWAY	Edwin	129	15	29/04/1870	Kingswood	S	Weaver	Stealing money	11d Imprisonment	Kingswood			1
M	SHORT	Nelson Daniel	B696	18	10/29/02	Cheltenham		Gardener	Stealing £1 in money	1 cal month HL	Cheltenham	CoE		4
M	SHOVELL	William											See A Williams	2
M	SIMMONDS	William	142	27	03/05/1870	Bristol	S	Baker	Embezzlement	1m Hard Labour	Westbury on Trym			1
F	SIMMONS	Maria	38		29/12/1887								Transferred from B'ham. B'ham Reg. No. 1112	2
M	SIMSON	Thomas	680		6/7/05									2
M	SIRRELL	Walter	134	30	29/04/1870	Almondsbury	M	Labourer	Stealing ducks	8m Hard Labour	Bristol		Previous: Highway Robbery with violence	1
M	SKERRETT	Jason	195		08/10/1892									2

Album	Sex	Surname	Forenames	Ref. No.	Age	Date of Photo	Birthplace	Marital	Occupation	Offence	Sentence	Destination	Religion	Notes
4	M	SKIPP	George Frederick	529	56	8/19/04	Gloster		Engineer	Stealing knife, spoon, bread & jacket	12 cal months HL		CoE	
4	M	SLACK	James	A992		15/06/1899								
2	M	SMALLMAN	George	555		18/09/1899								
1	M	SMITH	Alfred	249	19	11/06/1870	Gloucester	S	Sailmaker	Stealing wearing apparel	12w Hard Labour	Swindon, WIL		
2	M	SMITH	Charles	351		27/07/1887								
2	M	SMITH	Charles	3021		01/04/1884								
4	M	SMITH	Edward	B1013	24	1/31/02	London		Labourer	Stealing 2 pairs of boots	14 days HL		CoE	
4	M	SMITH	Edward	C990	27	1/12/03	Islington		Bootmaker	Stealing a silver watch from the person	5 years Penal Servitude		CoE	Alias FARLEY & KEMP
4	M	SMITH	Frederick	B109	32	8/12/02	Cheltenham		Labourer	Stealing 3 pairs of trousers	18 months HL		CoE	
4	M	SMITH	Frederick	A1042		4/17/1900								
4	M	SMITH	Frederick	A299		11/1/1900								
2	M	SMITH	Fredk.	4400		30/12/1884								Not in Index
4	M	SMITH	George	B1032	21	9/25/03	Gloucester		Labourer	Shopbreaking & stealing therein 56 metal 1lb checks	6 months HL	Gloucester	CoE	
1	M	SMITH	Henry	235	12	21/05/1870	Barnwood	S	Labourer	Stealing money	5d Hard Labour & 9 strikes with birch rod	Gloucester		
1	M	SMITH	Henry	48	32	30/04/1870	Wiltshire	M	Labourer	Stealing machine bands	1y Hard Labour	Bristol		
2	M	SMITH	Henry	191		3/22/04								See Henry Herbert
2	M	SMITH	Henry	279		08/05/1896								See WHITE
2	M	SMITH	James	9		2/1/04								
1	M	SMITH	John	253	18	18/06/1870	Leckhampton	S	Wheelwright	Burglary	6m Hard Labour	Leckhampton		
4	M	SMITH	John	B1108	18	5/5/02	Cheltenham		Labourer	Shopbreaking and stealing therein £1 12s 1d	6 weeks HL		CoE	
2	M	SMITH	John	44		26/09/1892								
2	M	SMITH	John	195		19/07/1893								
4	M	SMITH	Philip	B1074		6/10/02								
2	M	SMITH	Richard	IP893		07/11/1889								
4	M	SMITH	Robert	C1116	44	9/17/03	Bushton, WIL		Painter	Exposing his person; incorrigible rogue	HL till Q Sessions; 6 months		Wesleyan	Alias Oliver Selwyn
4	M	SMITH	Robert	C744	45	3/29/04	Bushton, WIL		Painter	Incorrigible rogue; exposing his person	6 months HL and 12 strokes with birch rod		Wesleyan	

Album	Sex	Surname	Forenames	Ref. No.	Age	Date of Photo	Birthplace	Marital	Occupation	Offence	Sentence	Destination	Religion	Notes
2	M	SMITH												
2	M	SMITH	Samuel	449		7/1/01								Alias RUDGE
2	M	SMITH	Sidney	320		28/06/1890								Apprehended Minchinhampton
1	M	SMITH	Thomas	262	26	25/06/1870	Minchinhampton	M	Labourer	Horse Stealing	12m Hard Labour	Stroud		
2	M	SMITH	Thomas	259		29/02/1888								GQ/834
2	M	SMITH	Thomas	GQ834		02/08/1890								3GS / 491
2	M	SMITH	Thomas	ZGS491		27/07/1892								
4	M	SMITH	William	B569	36	9/2/02	Weymouth		Labourer	Stealing a coat	21 days HL		CoE	Alias John WHITE
2	M	SMITH	William	163		11/09/1899								
2	M	SMITH	William	163		12/7/1900								Not in Index
1	M	SNOW	John	266	30	25/06/1870	Manchester	S	Miner	Stealing Shirts	1m Hard Labour	Uncertain, tramp		
1	M	SOUL	Andrew	182	40	03/05/1870	Turk Dean	M	Blacksmith	Stealing horse shoes	6w Hard Labour	Cheltenham		
1	M	SOULE	George	209	31	06/05/1870	Painswick	M	Shoemaker	Stealing coals	1m Hard Labour	Stonehouse		
4	M	SOUTHEY	Henry William	C675	18	10/13/03	Australia		Seaman	False pretences – goods	3 cal months HL		CoE	Alias Harry GREEN, and CARTER
Album	Sex	Surname	Forenames	Ref. No.	Age	Date of Photo	Birthplace	Marital	Occupation	Offence	Sentence	Destination	Religion	Notes
4	M	SPENCER	Ernest	C410	24	6/3/04	Huddersfield		Piano Tuner	Stealing a bicycle value £12 12s as bailee	3 months HL		Quaker	Alias Samuel SMITH
1	F	SPENCER	Hannah	109	22	30/04/1870	Cheltenham	S	Pauper	Stealing soap	7d Hard Labour	Cheltenham		
2	M	SPIERS	Richard	303		24/10/1886								
2	M	STALLARD	Arthur	504		04/08/1894								
4	M	STANLEY	Herbert	B386	19	10/28/01	Overbury, WOR		Labourer	Stealing a bicycle	1 Cal month HL		CoE	
1	M	STANTON	Solomon	14	18	20/12/1870	Cheltenham	S	Gardener	Stealing fowls	2m Hard Labour	Cheltenham		
2	M	STEPHENS	Arthur	74		07/12/1897								
4	M	STEPHENS	Frederick Henry	B423	38	10/24/02	Gloster		Labourer	Obtaining a suit of clothes by false pretences	1 cal month HL		CoE	
1	F	STEPHENS	Sarah	165	15	03/05/1870	Cirencester	S	Mendicant	Stealing wearing apparel	14d Hard Labour & R	Cheltenham		
2	M	STEPHENS	Thomas	245		16/10/1888								
1	M	STEPHENS	William	132	17	29/04/1870	Cheltenham	S	Labourer	Stealing a duck	10d Hard Labour	Cheltenham		
2	M	STERRY	C	524		4/5/06								Not in Index
4	M	STOKES	Henry	B979	44	2/14/02	Salisbury		Labourer	Stealing a bag & 7 fowls	1 month HL		CoE	
4	M	STONE	James	C415	28	8/6/03	Canning Town, Essex		Groom	Stealing a coat and vest	12 months HL & 3 years police supervision		CoE	Alias James WALKER

Album	Sex	Surname	Forenames	Ref. No.	Age	Date of Photo	Birthplace	Marital	Occupation	Offence	Sentence	Destination	Religion	Notes
4	M	STONE	James M A	B415	28	8/28/02	Canning Town, ESS			Breaking into a railway station & stealing money;	12 cal months HL		CoE	Alias james WALKER
2	F	STOREY	Sarah Ann	72		3/17/05								or BERRY
2	M	STRATTON	Weston											See Barton
1	M	STYLES	William	28	40	30/04/1870	Kent	S	Stone sawyer	Stealing Lindsey (Linseed?)	1m Hard Labour	Uncertain (a tramp)		
2	F	SULLIVAN	Jane											See BARRETT
2	M	SULLIVAN	John											See BARRETT
2	M	SURRIDGE	Thos.	684		14/04/1896								
4	M	SUTHERLAND	Frank	B572	25	10/4/01	Leeds		Ship's Cook	Stealing a coat and waistcoat	21 days HL		CoE	
1	M	SUTTON	William	85	13	30/04/1870	Tewkesbury	S	None	Stealing pistols	21d Hard Labour	Tewkesbury		
2	M	SWANN	William											
2	M	SYMONDS	Alfred	667		24/07/1895								
4	M	TAFT	James E	A404		2/5/1900								
2	M	TAYLOR	Albert	Q197		19/07/1890								Q/197
1	M	TAYLOR	Alfred	282	14	09/07/1870	Thornbury	S	Labourer	Stealing Rabbits	10d Hard Labour	Oldland Common		
2	M	TAYLOR	Andrew	479		3/5/06								
2	F	TAYLOR	Elizabeth	53		03/11/1890								
2	F	TAYLOR	Elizabeth	21		25/03/1893								
2	F	TAYLOR	Elizabeth	70		20/09/1898								
1	M	TAYLOR	Ephraim	152	18	03/05/1870	Cheltenham	S	Labourer	Stealing a duck	1m Hard Labour	Cheltenham		
4	M	TAYLOR	Frederick	B211	20	4/15/02	Hawthorne, Drybrook		Soldier	Indecent assault	12 months HL		CoE	
2	M	TAYLOR	Henry	207		12/14/01								
2	M	TAYLOR	James	640		5/1/03								
2	M	TAYLOR	John	163		13/07/1889								
2	M	TAYLOR	John	CIC329		07/11/1889								
1	M	TAYLOR	Samuel	281	18	09/07/1870	Thornbury	S	Labourer	Stealing Rabbits	10d Hard Labour	Oldland Common		
4	M	TAYLOR	William	C704	23	3/29/04	Chesterfield		Labourer	Housebreaking	6 cal months HL		CoE	
4	M	TAYLOR	William	B734	38	4/25/02	Prestbury		Hawker	Stealing a mare, dog, rug, etc	4 cal months HL		CoE	
4	M	TENNANT	Alfred Horatius	B633	17	10/29/02	Reading		Draper's Assistant	Stealing a bicycle	4 weeks HL		Wesleyan	
2	M	TETSELL	William	639		3/20/03									or TUTSELL
2	M	THOMAS	Arthur											See Fonier KING
2	M	THOMAS	George Heantry?											See Harry PAGE

Album	Sex	Surname	Forenames	Ref. No.	Age	Date of Photo	Birthplace	Marital	Occupation	Offence	Sentence	Destination	Religion	Notes
1	M	THOMAS	Henry	116	15	30/04/1870	Wickwar		Labourer	Stealing sweets				
4	M	THOMPSON	Edward	565	63	24/04/1899	Bristol		Tailor	Stealing a purse and 5s 2d from the person	18 cal months HL		CoE	
4	M	THOMPSON	Henry	B97	24	6/8/01	Southampton		Labourer	Assaulting one Sidney Timbrell	1 Cal. Month HL		CoE	
1	M	THOMPSON	John	168	36	03/05/1870	Scotland	M	Engine driver	Stealing tools	9m Hard Labour	Birmingham		Was in Scottish Greys
2	M	THORN	Robert	241		01/01/1892								
4	M	THORNHILL	Edward	A57		8/21/01								
2	M	THORNTON	Frank											See Fonier KING
4	M	THORNTON	William	B497	29	8/30/02	Manchester	S	ironworker	Stealing an overcoat	14 days HL	East Dean	CoE	
1	M	THURNEY	Charles	180	14	03/05/1870	Walford, HEF		Collier	Stealing money	5w Hard Labour			
1	M	TILEY	Richard	194	26	06/05/1870	Marshfield	M	Labourer	Stealing a purse and money	3m Hard Labour	Marshfield		
1	F	TILLING	Mary	170	32	03/05/1870	Kingscote	S	Servant	Stealing wearing apparel	2m Hard Labour	Cheltenham		
2	M	TILTON	George	539		01/01/1895		S						
1	F	TIPPER	Ellen	179	22	03/05/1870	Stafford	S	Servant	Burglary	8m Hard Labour	Worcester		
2	M	TITCH	Henry	289		9/16/04								
4	M	TOBIN	Joseph	B474	39	9/10/01	York		Labourer	Stealing a pair of boots	14 days or pay £1 15s		RC	
1	M	TOMMING	Thomas	214	18	07/05/1870	Birmingham	S	Blacksmith	Stealing money	6w Hard Labour	Birmingham		Alias Henry Phillips
4	M	TREEBY	John	C166	34	11/3/03	Plymouth		Shoemaker	Warehouse breaking and stealing boots and leather uppers	5 cal months HL		CoE	
4	M	TRESSIKER	Thomas	623	31	18/09/1899	Cornwall		Labourer	Burglariously breaking into a dwelling house & stealing therein one gold watch, one clock, one cloth cap	12 cal months HL		CoE	
4	M	TRIPP	James	B713	34	1/20/02	Charterhouse		Labourer	Obtaining 2s 6d by false pretences	3 months HL		CoE	Page Number under photo
4	M	TUCKER	Alfred Henry	B1247	36	3/31/02	Bristol		Porter	Setting fire to a stable and barn	See Assizes 15 Nov 1902		CoE	
4	M	TUDHOPE	George	776	30	10/11/04	Scotland		Watchman	Attempted suicide	7 days		CoE	
2	M	TUDOR	Henry	553		01/08/1894								
2	M	TUDOR	Henry	133		5/25/1900								
2	M	TURNER	John	328		12/1/05								
2	M	TURNER	John	624		2/20/03								
2	M	TURNER	John	99		7/18/05								

Album	Sex	Surname	Forenames	Ref. No.	Age	Date of Photo	Birthplace	Marital	Occupation	Offence	Sentence	Destination	Religion	Notes
2	M	UNDERWOOD	John	45		31/12/1889								John Brown or Stephen GOULDINGor Annie HOLLOWAY or Annie JONES
2	M	Unknown												
2	M	Unknown												Elizabeth JONES or Harriet JONES
4	M	VALLYATT	Emile	C36	45	7/7/03	Paris		Baker	Stealing two motor car lamps	1 cal month HL		RC	
2	M	VAUGHAN	John Arthur	3		6/19/03								
2	M	VAUGHAN	John Arthur	390		9/16/04								
2	M	VAUGHAN	Joseph	2428		02/10/1883								
2	M	VAUGHAN	Joseph	396		02/03/1887								
2	M	VAUGHAN	Joseph	461		05/11/1888								
2	M	VAUGHAN	Joseph	280		01/07/1891								
2	M	VAUGHAN	Thomas											(Missing photo?)
2	M	VAUGHAN	William	137		12/23/04								
2	M	VEDMORE	Henry											
2	M	VEDMORE	Henry	221		17/02/1887								
1	F	VERRIER	Charlotte	75	18	30/04/1870	Cheltenham	S	Servant	Stealing brooches	1m Hard Labour	Cheltenham		
1	M	VICKS	Charles	64	30	30/04/1870	Huntley	M	Engine Driver	Stealing a spoon	1m Hard Labour	Aston Ingham		
2	M	VINCENT	Gerald											See A Williams
1	M	WAINE	Joseph	151	17	03/05/1870	Cheltenham	S	Labourer	Stealing a duck	1m Hard Labour	Cheltenham		
2	M	WAINWRIGHT	George	35		04/06/1870								Missing
1	M	WAITES	William Henry	241	29	10/21/01	[Blank]	[Blank]	Groom	Stealing book	14d Hard Labour	Ross		
4	M	WALFORD	Richard	B580	60	10/18/02	Lydbrook		Coal dealer	Attempted suicide	10 days HL		Dissenter	
4	M	WALKER	Albert	B725	19		Wolverhampton		Labourer	Stealing 9s 6d, 1 silver watch & chain, one gold ring, one trinket, etc	2 months HL		CoE	Alias Albert BROOKS
1	M	WALKER	Alfred John	133	18	29/04/1870	London	S	Labourer	Stealing a duck	10d Hard Labour	Cheltenham		
2	M	WALKER	Frederick	572		9/29/04								
2	M	WALL	Francis	153		12/1/05								See J HOPSON
2	M	WALL	William											
1	M	WALLBRIDGE	Robert	113	36	30/04/1870	Hampshire	M	Labourer	Stealing a dog	3m Hard Labour	Lechlade		
2	M	WALSH	John	201		10/19/01								
2	M	WAITON	Amos	P198		16/12/1880								Not in Index

Album	Sex	Surname	Forenames	Ref.No.	Age	Date of Photo	Birthplace	Marital	Occupation	Offence	Sentence	Destination	Religion	Notes
4	M	WARD	John	B1105	24	2/25/02	Cardiff		Labourer	Stealing 2 overcoats	4 cal months HL		CoE	
4	M	WARD	John	1105	24	7/15/02	Cardiff		Labourer	Stealing two overcoats	4 cal months HL		CoE	
4	F	WARD	Mary	A132		11/12/1899								Photo sent to Norwich police, 28 Jun 1901
4	F	WARD	Mary			1899								
2	M	WARD	Thomas	334		30/06/1894								See MORRIS
2	M	WARNER	Henry	481		3/5/06								
2	M	WARNER	Henry											
4	M	WATKINS	Arthur Thomas	C355	32	6/20/03	Monmouthshire		Collier	Stealing a bicycle	10 cal months HL, 3 years Police Supervision		Wesleyan	
2	M	WATKINS	George	797		03/08/1897								
2	M	WATKINS	George									Newnham		
1	F	WATKINS	Mary Ann	153	21	03/05/1870	Manchester	S	Charwoman	Stealing coal	1m Hard Labour			
4	M	WATSON	Arthur	B357	30	8/12/01	Hendsford?, STS		Labourer	Stealing a bicycle	3 months HL		CoE	
2	M	WATSON	Edwin	73		18/04/1893								
2	M	WATSON	Harry	690		10/28/03								
2	F	WATTS	Emily	4		27/03/1886								
4	M	WATTS	Gregory John	C217	44	1/22/04	Oxford		Commission Agent	Obtaining £3 7s by false pretences	8 cal months HL		RC	
4	M	WEBB	Arthur Clifford	C344	30	7/7/03	Abergavenny		Compositor	Fraudulent conversion of money received on account of other persons	1 month HL		CoE	
2	M	WEBB	Thomas											(Missing Photo?)
1	M	WEBLEY	James	267	22	25/06/1870	Dymock	S	Labourer	Stealing Scythe	7d Hard Labour	Dymock		
4	F	WEEKS	Rose	A622		11/1/1900								Or Cooper
2	M	WELSH	John			01/05/1889								
2	M	WENT	Alfred	440		2/25/02								
4	M	WEST	Arthur	B1104	36	2/25/02	Devonport		Labourer	Stealing 2 overcoats	3 years PS		CoE	
2	M	WEST	Samuel	857		07/10/1895								
2	M	WHEELER	Henry	311		3/17/05								5 years. PS. Worcester Less 19/06/1905
1	F	WHEELER	Kate	208	16	06/05/1870	Leamington	S	None	Stealing blanket	3m Hard Labour	Cheltenham		
1	M	WHEELER	Mark	277	56	02/07/1870	Thornbury	M	Labourer	Stealing Timber	6m Hard Labour & 7y Police Supervision	Gloucester		

2	M	WHITE	Alfred	510		11/8/1900								Or Johnson or (Auves/Cleeves?)
2	M	WHITE	Alfred	510		2/11/01								Died in hospital 13/08/1901
4	M	WHITE	Arthur	C991	26	1/12/03	London		Painter	Stealing a silver watch from the person	5 years Penal Servitude		CoE	
4	M	WHITE	Ernest	C745	28	7/7/03	Kingswood, Bristol		Bootmaker	Stealing leather	9 months HL		CoE	
1	M	WHITE	George	67	15	30/04/1870	Gloucester	S	Labourer	Stealing books	20d Hard Labour	Gloucester		
4	M	WHITE	George	B41	46	5/6/02	Edmonton, MDX		Miner	Wilfully damaging a window	2 cal months HL		CoE	
2	M	WHITE	George											See SMITH
4	F	WHITE	Rose	A809		4/30/01								
1	M	WHITE	Samuel	71	26	30/04/1870	Cheltenham	M	Labourer	Stealing lead	2m Hard Labour	Cheltenham		
4	M	WHITE	Thomas	731	42	15/06/1899	Oxford		Gardener	Stealing a police sergeant's overcoat, helmet and belt	6 cal months HL & 3 years police supervision		CoE	Alias Charles Sylvester
2	F	WHITTAKER	Mary Ann	4189		07/01/1884								
1	M	WICKS	John	173	38	03/05/1870	Thornbury	S	Labourer	Stealing hay	2m Hard Labour	Newland		
4	M	WILCOX	Stephen	C223	19	10/9/03	[Blank]		Tailor	Stealing a bicycle	4 cal months HL		CoE	
Album	Sex	Surname	Forenames	Ref. No.	Age	Date of Photo	Birthplace	Marital	Occupation	Offence	Sentence	Destination	Religion	Notes
4	M	WILKES	Henry	B534	22	3/27/02	Gloster		Soldier	Stealing money & jewellery	6 cal months HL		CoE	
1	F	WILKES	Mary	163	34	03/05/1870	Norton	M	Field Worker	Stealing bacon	14d Hard Labour	Cheltenham		
2	M	WILLIAMS	Alfred	689		10/16/06								
2	M	WILLIAMS	Alfred	113		16/07/1889								
2	M	WILLIAMS	Charles	1		8/17/03								Not in Index
1	M	WILLIAMS	David	199	19	05/05/1870	Gloucester	S	Gardener	Stealing meal	2m Hard Labour	Gloucester		
2	M	WILLIAMS	David	304		13/04/1885								
2	M	WILLIAMS	Frederick	184		18/04/1892								Q/198
2	M	WILLIAMS	Frederick	565		10/27/02								
2	M	WILLIAMS	George	492		14/10/1887								
2	M	WILLIAMS	George											See George JONES
2	M	WILLIAMS	Henry	J45		17/03/1893								? 93.45
2	M	WILLIAMS	Henry											See Richard BIRD
4	M	WILLIAMS	Henry	A553		11/6/1900								
4	M	WILLIAMS	Henry	A553		11/26/01								

Album	Sex	Surname	Forenames	Ref. No.	Age	Date of Photo	Birthplace	Marital	Occupation	Offence	Sentence	Destination	Religion	Notes
2	M	WILLIAMS	James	419	24	08/03/1894	Manchester		Seaman	Stealing purse and money from the person	3 months HL		CoE	
4	M	WILLIAMS	John	772	28	9/29/04	London		Seaman	False Pretences	9 cal months HL		CoE	
4	M	WILLIAMS	John	C649	44	6/14/04	Huntley	M	Shoemaker	Stealing a pole	21d Hard Labour	Taynton		See Robert McKENZIE
1	M	WILLIAMS	John	29		30/04/1870								Not in Index
2	M	WILLIAMS	John	341		21/01/1887								
2	M	WILLIAMS	John	791		19/07/1888								
2	F	WILLIAMS	John Henry	83	52	30/04/1870	Plymouth	M	Servant	Cheat	1m Hard Labour	St George, GLS		
1	M	WILLIAMS	Mary											
2	F	WILLIAMS	Morris	9		09/01/1885								
2	M	WILLIAMS	My. Ann	146	66	03/05/1870	Cheltenham	M	Shoemaker	Stealing boots	1y Hard Labour	Birmingham		
1	M	WILLIAMS	Thomas	469		12/7/1900								Not in Index
2	M	WILLIAMS	Thomas	180		18/09/1899								
2	M	WILLIAMS	William Daniel	B292	18	7/26/01	Kidderminster		Striker	Stealing £2 10s the money of Abraham Matthews	1 cal. month HL		CoE	
4	M	WILLIFORD	William Henry	228	22	14/05/1870	Norton	S	Labourer	Stealing fowl	1m Hard Labour	Norton		
1	M	WILLIFORD	Richard	198	25	06/05/1870	Norton	S	Labourer	Stealing a fowl	1w Hard Labour	Norton		
1	M	WILLIS	Charles junior	95	17	28/04/1870	Westbury on Severn	S	Labourer	Horse stealing	6m Hard Labour	Westbury on Severn		
4	F	WILSON	Cath	A509		11/1/1900								
1	F	WILSON	Elizabeth	156	21	03/05/1870	Plymouth	M	Tramp	Stealing wearing apparel	6m Hard Labour	Uncertain		
1	F	WILSON	Emma	157	19	03/05/1870	Plymouth	S	Prostitute/tramp	Stealing wearing apparel	6m Hard Labour	Uncertain		
4	M	WILSON	George	B239	44	8/19/01	Boddingtons, Northants		Labourer	Indecent Assault	4 cal months HL		CoE	
1	M	WILSON	Walter	155	24	03/05/1870	Plymouth	M	Shoemaker/Tramp	Stealing wearing apparel	6m Hard Labour	Uncertain		
1	M	WILTSHIRE	John	32	67	30/04/1870	Somersetshire	S	Labourer	Stealing coal	14d Hard Labour	Bristol		
1	F	WINDOWS	Delina	81	22	30/04/1870	Westbury on Severn	S	Servant	Cheat	1m Hard Labour	Churcham		
4	M	WINDSOR	John	A891		6/22/1900								
1	M	WINGROVE	Henry	259	48	25/06/1870	Leith	S	Cabinet Maker	Stealing bottle of porter	10d Hard Labour	Thornbury		

Album	Sex	Surname	Forenames	Ref. No.	Age	Date of Photo	Birthplace	Marital	Occupation	Offence	Sentence	Destination	Religion	Notes
1	M	WINNIATT	Henry	1	45	19/04/1870	Bristol			Stealing an overcoat	6m Hard Labour & 1y Penal Servitude	Bristol		
2	M	WINSTONE	Walter	345		23/07/1885								
2	M	WITHERS	John	408		12/9/02								
2	M	WOOD	Arthur Edwin	139		9/10/03								
1	F	WOOD	Ellen	206	15	06/05/1870	Newnham	S	Servant	Stealing postage stamps	1m Hard Labour	East Dean		
1	M	WOOD	Thomas	98	14	29/04/1870	Stafford	S	Errand Boy	Stealing a lanthorn	20d Hard Labour	Gloucester		
4	M	WOOD	Walter James	C644	18	1/4/04	Cheltenham		Labourer	Housebreaking	3 cal months HL		CoE	
2	M	WOOD	William	167		15/07/1893								
2	M	WOODHOUSE	James	522		7/28/03								
1	M	WOOKEY	George	188	60	06/05/1870	Somerset	S	Labourer	Indecent assault	6m Hard Labour	Bitton		
4	M	WORGAN	George Frederick	B756	24	11/28/02	Chepstow		Labourer	Stealing clothing from a vessel	1 month HL		RC	
1	M	WORKMAN	Rufus	117	14	30/04/1870	Kingswood	S	None	Stealing sweets	10d Imprisonment & R	Kingswood		
2	M	WRIGHT	Arthur	126		9/4/03								
1	F	WYATT	Harriet Hancock	221	23	07/05/1870	Southampton	S	Tramp	Cheat	1m Hard Labour	Lower Norwood		
2	M	WYNDE	Francis	795		7/18/05								
4	F	YATES	Harriet	C790	30	11/3/03	Newent		None	Stealing boots	1 cal month HL		Baptist	
1	F	YEATES	Margaret	33	42	30/04/1870	Ireland	M	None	Stealing meat	10d Hard Labour	Campden		
4	M	YOUNG	Adolphus D	A909		6/22/1900								
4	M	YOUNG	Adolphus Daniel	B518	22	5/6/02	Stroud		Labourer	Indecent assault; obstructing police	8 cal months HL		CoE	
1	M	YOUNG	John	271	30	02/07/1870	Wilts	S	Labourer	Stealing Boots	6m Hard Labour & 7y Police Supervision	Bath		

BIBLIOGRAPHY

Hawkins, David T. (1992), *Criminal Ancestors*, Stroud, Sutton Publishing Ltd.

Howard, John (1929) *The State of the Prisons*, London, J.M. Dent & Sons.

Kear, Averil (2002) *Bermuda Dick*, Lydney, Lightmoor Press.

One Who Has Endured it (1877) *Five Years Penal Servitude*, London, Richard Bentley & Son.

Priestley, Philip (1999) *Victorian Prison Lives,* London, Pimlico.

Documents Accessed

The following documents relating to Gloucester Gaol and held in Gloucestershire Archives were referenced:

Q/Gc/3 Governor's Journals.

Q/Gc/6 Registers of Prisoners 1844 – 1879.

Q/Gc/9 Registers of Summary Convictions.

Q/Gc/10 Duplicate returns of habitual criminals and albums of prisoners' photographs.

Q/Gc/12 Nominal prisoners' registers.

Q/Gc/13 Record of previous convictions.

Q/Gc/14 After trial calendars of prisoners, Quarter Sessions and Assizes.

Q/Gc/31 Chaplain's Journals.

Other titles published by The History Press

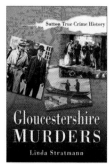

Gloucestershire Murders
LINDA STRATMANN

Contained within the pages of this book are the stories behind some of the most notorious murders in Gloucestershire's history. The cases covered here record the county's most fascinating but least known crimes, as well as famous murders that gripped not just Gloucestershire but the whole nation.

978 0 7509 3950 8

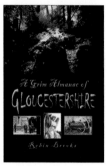

A Grim Almanac of Gloucestershire
ROBIN BROOKS

This alternative look at Gloucestershire's past provides a day-by-day journey through the grim underbelly of the county's history, looking at crimes and misdemeanours, strange natural phenomena, folk tales and curious customs.

978 0 7509 3538 8

Prison Life in Victorian England
MICHELLE HIGSS

Find out what life in prison was really like for the Victorian convict and prisoner, and also for the prison officers who looked after them. Using original prison records, contemporary sources and testimony from convicts, prisoners and prison officers, this book examines every aspect of the Victorian English prison to bring this fascinating period of social history to life.

978 0 7524 4255 6

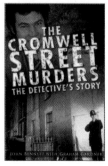

The Cromwell Street Murders: The Detective's Story
ANGELA BENNETT

The full story of how the Wests were caught, how the case was prepared and how it nearly failed to come to court, by the officer in charge of the investigation. This chronicles the roles of those who brought down two of Britain's most infamous killers, shedding light on the real heroes of one of the saddest chapters of criminal history. The book explores the court processes and the various complications of Rose West's trial.

978 0 7509 4385 8

Visit our website and discover thousands of other History Press books.
www.thehistorypress.co.uk